Spousal Grief

How I Survived the First 12 Months

Kylie Wood

First published by Ultimate World Publishing 2025
Copyright © 2025 Kylie Wood

ISBN

Paperback: 978-1-923425-01-9
Ebook: 978-1-923425-02-6

Kylie Wood has asserted her rights under the Copyright, Designs and Patents Act 1988 to be identified as the author of this work. The information in this book is based on the author's experiences and opinions. The publisher specifically disclaims responsibility for any adverse consequences which may result from use of the information contained herein. Permission to use information has been sought by the author. Any breaches will be rectified in further editions of the book.

All rights reserved. No part of this publication may be reproduced, stored in or introduced into a retrieval system, or transmitted in any form, or by any means (electronic, mechanical, photocopying, recording or otherwise) without the prior written permission of the author. Any person who does any unauthorised act in relation to this publication may be liable to criminal prosecution and civil claims for damages. Enquiries should be made through the publisher.

Cover design: Ultimate World Publishing
Layout and typesetting: Ultimate World Publishing
Editor: James Salmon
Cover Image Copyright: jadimages-Shutterstock.com

Ultimate World Publishing
Diamond Creek,
Victoria Australia 3089
www.writeabook.com.au

Dedication

To my person Ryan.

I knew you best, I loved you most, I feel your absence the greatest.

I got to be your happily ever after and I'm truly grateful.

Forever 51

Contents

Dedication	iii
Introduction: It Wasn't Meant To Be This Way	1
Chapter 1: Alone in the Unknown	5
Chapter 2: Sending Up the Flare	23
Chapter 3: Grief Is the Shadow of Love	33
Chapter 4: The Weight of New Beginnings	47
Chapter 5: A World Without You	57
Chapter 6: Living in the Grip of PTSD	67
Chapter 7: Standing at the Crossroads	77
Chapter 8: Seeking Sunshine in the Shadows	87
Chapter 9: Healing Begins With You	103
Chapter 10: The Quiet Reminders of Love	111
Chapter 11: Putting a Name to the Pain	125
Chapter 12: The Year That Changed Everything	135
Reflection	145
About the Author	147

Introduction

It Wasn't Meant To Be This Way

Wednesday 18th October 2023 will be etched in my memory forever.

It was the worst day of my life.

It was the day I now realise I measure so much by, referring to life as 'Before' or 'After' that day.

It was the day my heart shattered into a million pieces.

It was the day he died.

I rewind for just a moment to the 29th August 2023. We boarded a plane from Brisbane, Australia to start our 'gap year'. We had

Spousal Grief

travelled to Dubai and Italy only three months earlier and upon our return home we talked about further travel. 'Let's spend 2024 overseas following the sun,' we said. Then it was 'Why are we waiting, let's do it now, life is too short'! How prophetic that turned out to be.

We were so happy. This was to be three months of travelling, home before Christmas, some domestic travel in early 2024 and off again overseas to continue our year of us.

But Wednesday 18th October 2023 put a stop to all that.

After waking up in our Airbnb apartment in Porto, Portugal to him saying he 'didn't feel right', I rolled over to flick the beside lamp on and turned back to see the life ripped from his body. It was so quick, so final.

Who is he?

His name is Ryan and he is my person, the one I chose to live life with into old age, the one I naively thought would be around for the rest of my life. Instead, I was the person he shared the rest of his life with.

Losing your person is a great shock no matter the circumstances. Being in a foreign country having the time of your lives and losing them is incomprehensible.

Time seemed to move so slowly but so fast all at once. Calling the ambulance, asking to speak to someone who spoke English, putting Ryan in the recovery position, calling out for help and

It Wasn't Meant To Be This Way

banging on doors to the other apartments. As luck would have it, Australian doctors on holiday in a neighbouring apartment heard my shouts and came to Ryan's aid, but they couldn't revive him. The paramedics arrived 16 minutes 38 seconds after my call, but they couldn't save him. The apartment filled up with police, the coroner and then they all slowly left as their jobs were done.

And I was left alone.
Alone to make phone calls to my children, my best friend, his family.
Alone to pack up our things into our suitcases.
Alone to call the Airbnb host to ask for assistance.
Alone to call a hotel to find a safe space to try to make sense of what the hell had just happened.
Alone to call the Australian Consulate.
Alone to call the Funeral Directors.
Alone to deal with the red tape that comes with a death overseas.
Alone.

We still had so much to see and do, together. This wasn't meant to happen.

This is where my latest and most difficult journey begins.

Chapter 1

Alone In The Unknown

<u>18th October 2023</u>

Ryan, the coroners have taken your body away. I am alone in our Airbnb apartment and I've called my boys to tell them what's happened. Jet, my youngest, wants to fly here, he's checked his bank account and said he has enough money to book a flight. Max, my oldest, is distressed that I am over the other side of the world on my own. I've told them I want them to stay home. Then I called Faye, my BFF, and sobbed. She wants to get on a plane too but I don't want that. I am ok on my own right now, I don't want people around me.

Spousal Grief

Now I have to phone your family. I am dreading that call, particularly given the way things are with your mother. So I take a deep breath and call and message your sister a number of times from both my phone and yours, wondering why she's not answering when she normally has her phone glued to her. I find out that she is on her way to the UK to see her daughter and she calls me from Dubai, but we have such poor reception and I am at my wit's end. In the end I break the news over Messenger and immediately she responds 'WTF' and miraculously finds better reception. Through my tears I explain what happened and I ask her to call your parents. I am worried that they're each on their own with no support. Your sister says she will call them tomorrow when she reaches England. I am annoyed and I know you'd be rolling your eyes, so I say, 'He is their son, they need to know now' and I tell her I'll do it.

I take another deep breath and call your mother. Of course I can't get through as we are not socially connected anymore. She calls me back and I break the awful news of your death and she yells at me!! Why am I not surprised? The last time I saw her she was yelling at me. I tell her to stop yelling, that I've done my duty to her and will now call your father. She backs off but I hang up even more upset.

Now for your dad, who can't ever operate his phone. I call a number of times from both our phones and eventually get through with some help from his neighbour downstairs. I say I am sorry to have to tell him you're gone and he kindly asks if I am ok. I am so grateful for his show of compassion. I am broken and I know he will be too. I finish the call as there's nothing else to say.

Alone In The Unknown

I'm aware I am now operating on auto pilot. I am in crisis mode, it's what I do best.

I call the Australian Consulate for assistance as I am really unsure what I am supposed to do, being a foreigner here. It seems complicated but they're so helpful explaining and confirming what the police have told me already.

We were meant to be leaving for Madrid tomorrow. I cannot stay in this apartment any longer. I throw all of our things into our suitcases and call the Airbnb hosts. They race to my aid. My upbringing and good manners kick in and through my tears I apologise that I have not cleaned out the fridge, that I am leaving early, that the bed is soiled, the list of mundane, unimportant things that roll off my tongue from inside my head. They reassure me that nothing is a problem and help me navigate a taxi, getting our suitcases into the car and with a big hug, a promise that they are available to help me in any way I need, the taxi speeds off to my new destination.

I walk into the hotel to check in and am met by the manager. I break down as I blurt out to him what has happened and finish with 'I don't know how long I need a room'. He is wonderful and smooths the way for me.

I speak with the funeral director and he comes to see me at the hotel. I have so many decisions to make but am confident in the information he provides as it lines up with what the police and the Consulate have told me. And I am thankful that you and I have spoken of our wishes in the event of our untimely death. And even though we differ in our personal requests, we trusted

Spousal Grief

each other implicitly and I will not let you down. I will honour what you want and not let anyone 'turn it into a circus' as you warned me could happen if you go first.

As evening arrives, I order room service, a bottle of wine and some food (no idea what) even though I am not hungry and I sit here numb. I am looking through photographs desperate to see your face and I am writing. Some of it makes sense, much of it doesn't, but all of it is helping in some small way. I feel so utterly alone but writing my thoughts and feelings to you is cathartic. It's like I am sending you a letter and you'll get to read it soon.

Faye rings and talks to me, she continues to do this morning and night for months on end. I can never ever thank her enough for her unwavering support even whilst she is also grieving your loss as her BFF's person and her friend.

I am looking at photos of you with some of our rescue kittens. I always knew you were a real man of great character by how you treat animals! You are the reason we have cats as part of our family. And because I take things to a whole new level we became involved in rescue and fostering. So you are to blame for this crazy cat lady. And out of every litter of needy kittens that came through our door there was always one who singled you out as her boyfriend. Every time I said there's another two or eight in need of care or a mum with babies or whatever, you supported me every single time. You did feeds, you emptied litter trays, you cleaned floors for these babies with no word of complaint. When you get to your next destination you'll be playing with all the cats and kittens and dogs and puppies and all manner of animals who have crossed the rainbow bridge and you'll be in your element showing them the love they deserve. But I am so sad that our future foster babies will miss out on knowing your physical presence; our past foster babies were blessed to have your love.

I see a photo of you with a huge smile and look of love on your face holding our wicked white witch Zima in the first few days after we rescued her years ago and it strikes me how it's the little things you don't miss until they're gone. Like sticking my finger in your adorable cheek dimple which always made you smile even wider and laugh at me for doing it.

Death is so final.

19th October 2023

I get up this morning and head down for breakfast, I figure I need something to sustain me and I fool myself into thinking I am strong enough to do this in a busy restaurant. After all, it's only breakfast, in a hotel, with a buffet. I've done it hundreds of times before. Boy was I wrong. I guess the staff had been given the heads up about me and the kindness I was shown broke me. People at the tables around me discreetly glanced over no doubt speculating about the woman on her own in tears with the waitress hugging her. The stares don't rattle me but I feel trapped and desperately need to get out of there and back to the safety of my room.

As I sit by the window looking out the window on another cold rainy day, man does the sun ever shine in this city, I spot a

Spousal Grief

familiar sign of a supermarket not far away. I need to get out. I put on the rain jacket and set my GPS walking directions and head off. As I enter the supermarket there's women handing out bags and requests for food donations to send aid to I can't recall where. It was a good distraction so I filled up the bag, added a bottle of wine, bag of chips and container of hummus for me, paid and left.

When I got back to the hotel there were flowers from Faye and Chris, a massage voucher, and the first of the daily fruit platters started arriving. I am sure the hotel were concerned I wasn't eating properly and every day I received a complimentary platter of fresh fruit.

I had a beautiful friend in Brisbane reach out and offer to do a long-distance healing for me. Such a kind and thoughtful gift and I am forever grateful for that. One thing that stood out from that reading was giving me the reminder and strength to say no. I knew I would need to draw on that in the coming days and weeks.

I drank half the wine and ate half the hummus and chips and didn't leave the room again.

Faye made her nightly call (her morning) and she calms me. I go to bed and ask you to help me sleep. I lay on my side and stare at the darkness, at some point I feel your hand on my hip, it gives me comfort and I fall asleep.

Alone In The Unknown

20th October 2023

It's been 48 hours since you spoke your last words to me in bed in the dark telling me, 'I don't feel right'. In the past those words put me on alert immediately and generally meant a trip to the hospital either in the car or by ambulance just to make sure, given you had a heart condition from your heart attack nine years before. This time you never heard my response asking what was wrong, what were you feeling, you never saw me jump to turn the light on, you never heard me yelling your name, you never felt my hands shaking you, turning you on your side, calling for help, you were already gone, all over in an instant. This time the ambulance came but you never had a chance, you had already left the building.

I rewind and cling to memories of the night before. We were like locals wandering up the road in our matching rain jackets to an exquisite little vegan restaurant right on our street. We got to share the best food we've had on this trip and even had room for dessert each, a rarity for us but the menu was too good not to. We drank cocktails then beer for you and wine for me, talked about our future plans and that we felt we were on the right path with those mutual dreams and goals. We laughed together. We were closer than ever. We were a team.

For lunch I drank the other half of the wine and ate more hummus and chips. My day consists of looking at photos, crying, dozing on repeat. I feel like I've been run over and left for dead.

It's now evening. You'd be proud babe, I put my big girl pants on and went down for dinner alone! Basically, hummus and

Spousal Grief

chips had run out in the room. Chef prepared a lovely impressive vegan meal and I had your favourite cocktail, a Mojito, and it was a good one! A romantic setting wasted without you. Miss you so much.

Back to the room alone I went.

21st October 2023

Ryan, I don't know if you realised, but quite often I would sit and gaze at your face and really study it, the laugh lines, the shape of your nose and cheeks, those dimples, your jawline, your blue eyes, the fullness of your bottom lip, your soft ears, the wrinkles creeping in, the grey in your hair. Because I love the beauty in your face. It was something I was drawn to do, not really knowing why but I always felt such love at the time. Now I know why. I was memorising it for this very time when I would need your face imprinted on my memory, for this time moving forward when I can no longer take for granted the blessing of seeing your face every morning when I wake up or at night before I fall asleep.

Today is going to be a tough one. You've started the next part of the journey of me getting you home, the coroner has released your physical body and the funeraries are preparing your beautiful face for me to physically see it one more time. Taking it one day at a time.

Your sister arrived in Portugal this afternoon with a friend in tow. That really upset me. The friend was a lovely lady who I understand you grew up with, and she was very respectful, but having a stranger thrust on me here in this nightmare was the last thing I wanted. This was happening with no discussion as to how I would feel about it. I didn't cause a scene, the peacemaker that I am, and I was still somehow thinking it was all a dream that I'd wake up from very soon.

Your sister was here for your viewing and for some reason thought I had arranged a cremation service. She handed me a lovely card with some beautiful words about us together and had written a letter to you which she placed in your open casket. She then asked me to book 'our favourite restaurant' for dinner and your mother wanted to pay. I find this insensitive, but when you've never lost a spouse then I suppose they're not considering that I cannot go back to the restaurant where we spent our last magical night together. That would be hell. So I choose another vegan restaurant we were going to try and hold it together through the pain of your absence.

22nd October 2023

Yesterday was the day I saw your physical body for the last time Ryan and that is all it was, a body, a shell, a lifeless stranger. It wasn't you. I had to put my foot down when your sister and her inevitable camera was brought out to photograph you. I knew how angry you would be at this, I could hear you in my ear and I used up one of my resounding NO's voicing your thoughts. This was one photo that was not going to happen.

So many emotions came to the surface as I leant over your body telling you how much I love you, but in the end three remained:

disconnection, anger and a deep sadness that you have been cheated out of fulfilling your future dreams. I feel like I am now standing on the outside looking in, waiting in limbo for something. But what?

So now I direct my thoughts and heart elsewhere. To the warmth you had, that I was lucky enough to see more than anyone, because you were not a physical person with others, expressing emotion to others didn't come naturally to you. You weren't totally comfortable with people encroaching into your personal space. It wasn't your love language. And as each day passes the realisation and the loss of your true personal love language of Acts of Service is felt more and more. Because you showed your love through the things you did without fuss or fanfare. You just did things that you thought would make me happy, would make it easier for me. You always had the best intentions, centred around seeing me happy. You cared enough to sacrifice your own time for not only my benefit but others you cared about. And that's not something you find in a person every day.

Thank you for sharing your unique form of love.

23rd October 2023

This morning as I wake up I feel a bit like the photo I took of us on the famous yellow Lisbon tram – you're not quite in focus, you've faded into the background a little bit and it's a distressing feeling but one that is only temporary as I wait in this holding pattern of government red tape to get you home. My thoughts are disjointed and not flowing, so rather than push against the tide I am just letting it be for now.

You weren't keen on being in photos, so I spend a lot of time scrolling through copious amounts of images looking for those that I forced or snuck you into so I can focus on the things I gained through our shared experiences, rather than the thought of what I've lost with your absence. And I do laugh at the faces you pulled and how sometimes you pushed back against being photographed and other times leaned into it just to make me happy or get me off your back – a fine line there. These are the memories I spoke to you about, that if you're not in the pictures then how do we even know you were there when we look back on our travels together! I see you scowl at me but you knew I was right.

I know I pushed you outside your comfort zone A LOT in the last eight years but in my eyes now it was worth every minute of discomfort, every eye roll, every mutter under your breath, as for a brief moment we got to live the life together we chose up until the end. Ironically, our motto this trip was 'Life's too short'! This was something we spoke out loud a few times laughing as we made last minute changes to itineraries and checked into luxury accommodation as the mood took us. Eerily prophetic!!

I shake it off for the time being as there's more to that thought that I am not ready to explore further just yet.

So …..

Spousal Grief

The funerary company here in Porto will have all the official paperwork completed today and tomorrow and will return your ashes to me on Wednesday. Thursday morning local time we fly out and will arrive home around midnight on Friday AEST.

At this stage I just want to get you home. Then I will focus my attention on a memorial service, maybe a paddle out to get you back into your beloved ocean. I don't know, I don't want the pressure of thinking about letting you go, it's too permanent. For now I just need to get us home.

24th October 2023

There's a definite pattern here since you've gone. I wake up around 4am and I am never surprised by the time nor by your absence. Then I cry. Then I hear your last words on repeat. Then the same random Sinead O'Connor song won't stop playing in my head. I think I have to stop it somehow. I then go back to sleep.

When I wake again this time I AM surprised you're not here and that's when I start flipping through memories until my brain latches onto one, like a lifeline. I have no control over which memory my mind settles on but it's mostly a happy one. And then it begins.

Today I remember how you always laughed at some of the strange things I do. And how it was never mean, it was more caring, to you it was funny and cute at the same time. That it was a uniqueness about me and you liked it. It made me more human to you because for a capable, controlled, intelligent woman I didn't

Alone In The Unknown

always appear so bright or carefree and vulnerable. I enjoyed the laughs it brought you.

I want to tell you about the other day. I went for a long walk, and I mean a loooong walk, from the hotel because I couldn't find a taxi. I met up with a social media friend who kindly reached out to me as she's in Porto now too. Such a beautiful soul to give me her time and a shoulder to cry on. You would have enjoyed the café I chose, it was all plant-based and really good. On the way back to the hotel I walked into a random church and lit about 30 candles for you and said a prayer. I sat and had a cry as tourists walked by snapping photos of yet another church interior and then I started laughing through the tears as I looked around at the scary morbid Jesus scenes knowing you would be thinking I'd lost the plot as you're definitely not a religious man.

I want to tell you about this evening, that I went down to dinner and sat openly listening to the two men at the next table, just like you would, and couldn't fathom how one of them had no idea what spaghetti bolognese or fettuccine carbonara was on the menu and they kept discussing the two dishes over and over again. I was ready to interrupt and ask what planet he had been living on and I can nearly hear you laughing saying, 'Go on babe, do it'.

And I want to desperately tell you about my massage yesterday, the one Faye organised for me. How as soon as the lady asked me if I was ok the tears started. She was so very kind. She then handed me the inevitable paper g-string as they do and left the room. Now the room was very dark and moody of course and in my defence I didn't have my glasses on. So I put the g-string

Spousal Grief

on and wriggled it and jiggled it and adjusted it and for the life of me I couldn't get it to sit right. So I just gave up. As I lay face down and she started the massage it dawned on me that I had put one leg through the waist so the micro triangle bit that should be pretending to cover my bum bits was actually sitting smack bang in the middle of one cheek. And I knew you would have lost it when I told you all about it.

But of course when I turn to tell you all of this you're not here to laugh along with me.

And then the song starts up in my head again and its truth shows up - Nothing Compares To You.

25th October 2023

How has it been a week already Ryan? A week since you last spoke to me. A week since the amazing Australian doctors on holiday in the next apartment heard me calling out and came to your aid. A week since that lovely little apartment was overflowing with strangers, medics, police, morgue assistants. A week since they told me in broken English that you were gone. A week since they took your body away and I was left with silence, a gaping hole where you had been.

I remember packing up your things, our things into our suitcases. The apartment hosts arriving, hugging me, calling me a taxi, helping me with our luggage. I remember unpacking at the hotel to try to gain some sense of normalcy. I then repacked your clothes into your suitcase. And over this past week I've unpacked them again. I've sorted through them, handing over clothing to the funerary people, putting aside the clothes you last wore. They still smell like you so I've packed them again to bring them home for Zima to sleep on. I've repacked the rest of your clothes into big white bags and I won't be unpacking them again.

I head out with the big white bags in tow to find a taxi to take me to the Red Cross donation centre where I hand over the bags of your clothing, imagining some local surfer thinking they've hit the jackpot with the surf brands you love so much. I handle it well until the taxi driver brings me back to the hotel and tells me he won't accept my money for driving me. He's an older man and he gives me a fatherly smile full of empathy and says some words of comfort in broken English. I break down and head into the hotel sobbing as I cross the lobby to the lifts to take me back upstairs.

Today is another of those tougher days. They will bring your ashes to me this afternoon and I'll work out how to 'pack you' for our journey home.

There's no voice on repeat today. There's no random song replaying. There's only silence and a great weariness.

I'll be glad to get out of here.

26th October 2023

What a terrible night's sleep I've had Ryan, my anxiety has been through the roof and I am exhausted. I haven't dreamt in a week so of course last night was the night that my brain went into overdrive again and my dreams were confused, disjointed, and so intense.

I am frantically looking on my phone for something to stop a panic attack and I see a photo of us earlier this year in Italy and I soften a little. My heart is still racing and my jaw is clenched tight but I start to relax. I am so glad that I surprised you that day with an upgrade on our flights. And I am so glad that I decided that we would always fly in style from that point forward. It's all part of the journey, the fun, the experience of each trip, it starts when you get on that plane. Life is too short!

You hadn't travelled very much until we met so you left the plans in my hands. And you stood at the airport that day in Italy with a very puzzled look on your face saying to me, 'That's the wrong line, that's business and first class, babe'. And I said, 'It will be ok, we'll just stand here'. And as always when I tried to buck the system you said, 'You can't do that' and I responded with, 'Why not!' Then you laughed, shook your head and shrugged your shoulders because you knew I was either on a mission or up to something and I'd show my hand eventually. And I loved that about you, even in times of discomfort or when you weren't sure what was happening in the end you let go and trusted me.

When you said you didn't care flying economy class as you could sleep anywhere, we – ok I – used to joke that I'd book myself up the front and see you at the other end. Your eyes would widen at me and you'd try to work out if I was joking. But you knew deep down I'd never do that, we were a team. And you loved flying in style, you loved staying in a nice hotel and I gave that to you too this trip. I am so glad I did.

Alone In The Unknown

So today we leave Portugal bound for home. And guess what babe, you're flying First Class with me! I only wish you'd got to do it in person and not in spirit. But such is this life, these cards we've been dealt.

Goodbye Porto, I wish we'd met under different circumstances.

I have two stopovers on this long flight home and the legs to Lisbon and onto Dubai are both Business Class. As I board the flight from Lisbon to Dubai with you in my hand luggage I find I am seated next to a young Indian gentleman who is putting his hand luggage in the overhead locker above our seats. I look in and find there is no room to place the bag carrying your ashes directly above me and he gestures to one of the other lockers further down the plane. I tell him no. He looks at me and shows me the overhead is full with his bag but there's room two rows ahead for me and again I say no. I become quite agitated and distraught over this simple task. I raise my voice and tell him firmly that you are travelling directly above me and nowhere else on this flight and he will need to move his bags. He must have wondered what brand of insanity I was packing, but he moved his bag to make way for me. I settle into my seat and quietly cry to myself, questioning yet again why why why!!

Dubai to Brisbane was First Class and I am so glad I made the decision to pay for the upgrade. Flying towards home set off another raging of emotions and I was able to close the door to my sleeping pod and deal with it all privately. The staff had no idea of our circumstances, but at one point one of the gentleman attendants said he had an overwhelming feeling that he needed to tell me that I was the kindest passenger he had ever had the

Spousal Grief

pleasure to assist. Another round of tears at his words, and he looked a bit concerned that he'd said the wrong thing. I then told him about your death and pointed to the bag containing your ashes. Empathy shone from his eyes, no words were needed, his fatherly presence was a blessing.

I remember looking out the window and seeing Australian land beneath me and I burst into tears. I never realised the impact seeing Australian soil below would have on me during this hardest experience of my life.

The next set of tears came as I navigated my way through customs. I declared your remains and went to show them the official documentation but was waved through very quickly. I don't think the young customs officer knew how to handle me to be honest. Through the tears I did briefly think that I could have been carrying anything then just as quickly dropped the thought as I headed out into the airport to find my pre-booked driver to take me home. A woman driver was a pleasant surprise and as she tried to take my luggage trolley from me I held tightly and burst into tears again saying I needed to stay in control of my bags. More kindness and empathy as she let me set the tone for the ride home.

Chapter 2

Sending Up the Flare

29th October 2023

Well we made it home last night after around 27 hours travelling. I'd purposely told my boys that I did not want to be met at the airport. I know myself better than anyone and knew I needed the time in the back of the car with a stranger at the wheel to decompress before facing them.

It's been an emotional roller coaster that's for sure. Whilst I expected tears at being home with my boys and the animals, what I didn't expect was the raw feeling of being back at day one and feeling I've lost you all over again.

Spousal Grief

I am totally overwhelmed and anxious, can't really sleep, and copious amounts of camomile tea have done nothing. So through the night last night I unpacked and discarded things as I went and tried to gain some sense of order.

The animals are another story. Jasper is indifferent, just wants a cuddle from anyone, Mila cried when she heard me crying, Murray is being a clingy weirdo as usual and our white witch Zima won't really come near me and instead stares menacingly at me from across the room with a look that says 'Where is my dad, you killed him didn't you!!'

It strikes me that this is one of those things you think happens to other people. And you feel sadness and compassion for them, those other people. But this time it has happened to us. We are those other people.

My beautiful niece has arranged meals for me all sitting in my fridge ready to eat and take that one important task off my list, sustenance. I am so very blessed by her thoughtfulness and kindness.

So today I've kept busy and the boys have helped get some things done that you would normally do.

This afternoon exhaustion caught up a little and I slept for a couple of hours. But upon waking the reality kicks in and I sob inconsolably all over again. And it surprises me yet again, it feels an insurmountable mountain of grief to climb over.

But that will change just as the seasons will change, in due time.

Until then I make more tea, I tick a to-do item off the list and I climb in and out of bed in an attempt to sleep.

Life sucks right now and I can only ride it out, there is no other way!

31st October 2023

Where do I start babe!

Yesterday was a pretty good day. I am starting to sleep so woke up a bit refreshed and on a mission. I spent the whole morning trying to sort out one item off the list. I never realised how emotionally draining it is when you have to keep repeating your story over and over again as you get bumped from department to department. You would think with such a sensitive call surrounding death and loss they'd soften the landing but it's not to be!

Then it was time to visit your dad. He was sad and we had some teary moments and some laughter. It was a good visit and it filled in some blanks for him about you, his son and his mate, that gave him some comfort whilst he mourns you.

Then I came home and slept and slept. Got up a couple of times but I had definitely hit a wall.

Spousal Grief

1st November 2023

After getting some decent sleep, this morning started out well. I had a 9am appointment at home and it was quite positive. Then I needed to find a Justice of the Peace to sign documents. I got in the car and headed down the road and that's when everything started falling apart. I got my errands done but I felt like I was walking through quicksand with each step heavier than the last.

Then that first wave rolled in and hit me head on and dragged me under. I've never felt so helpless in my life. Wave after wave of grief pounded me today until I gave in and sent up a flare, a call for help. I realised this was the day that I can't do this on my own any longer. Thank god for my BFF, that's true love and friendship right there. She booked a flight, left work and went home to pack and arrived not long ago. My lifeline is here and I am so grateful. The waves are still pounding but I can feel the tide is turning and I'll be safe once again.

Grief sucks the life out of those left behind. It has brought back the memory of the pain of losing my mum 25 years ago. That was shocking, unexpected just like now. I never ever imagined I would be feeling this again in this lifetime.

I miss you so much.

Tomorrow will be a better day.

Sending Up the Flare

3rd November 2023

I can't believe it, today is the day we were to embark on our river cruise from Lyon, France! It's where this trip planning of ours all started. I had stumbled upon the cruise and was so excited it was 100% vegan and you, as always, showed support for me and my lifestyle so I booked it. Then I planned our trip around it. We were so looking forward to this cruise, not having to navigate the lack of options in a non-vegan world, knowing that it was all done for us for a whole week. And we were so excited to see what the chefs would come up with, how the land tours would incorporate veganism, just living in a vegan cocoon for a short time was going to be utter bliss.

I haven't kept track of 'what should have been' as I plow daily through the red tape and to do lists following your passing and just now saw a notice about the cruise and looked at the date on the calendar.

I feel like I've been kicked in the stomach.

But it seems like such an insignificant thing.

In this moment I can't breathe.

I've been relatively dry eyed for most of the last two days.

The wave rises and hits me once more. Tears flow. They feel different. It's not the grief I've become familiar with as I am back to thinking you might walk through the door. It's more a sadness for what should be happening right now for us versus what is our reality.

Spousal Grief

My reality is re-learning how to do life without you.

It's not by choice, but what is the alternative!!

7th November 2023

So I did a thing this week Ryan! I made a big decision and made it happen. I bought a new house and will be selling the property.

I can see you smile and shake your head in good humour at how I make a decision and then make it happen very quickly even when I've got a million other things to contend with at the time. I can see your brain work through the packing up, what will be culled and what we will take with us. I can see you think about where the closest surf is to the new house. And you'd smile and nod your head at our new adventure. I know with great certainty that you would never question my timing, my thought process, my reasoning.

Of course some have opinions on whether I am making a hasty decision, others know this is what I do best, do some research and be decisive. It doesn't matter what anyone thinks, it's my sanity at stake and I know what's best for me right now. We had spoken about selling versus renovating so it's no surprise to me that I've chosen this path.

I look around here at our beautiful property up high on a hill with views all around from the ocean to the hinterland and all I see now are broken dreams, a reminder of what we were planning to do together. And I don't have the heart or energy for it. This project is already in the past, it died with you. It was part of us, not just me. And I am ok with that.

I am moving so I can find peace and work out how to heal.

I know you'd support me, you supported anything I did even if you had doubts. We'd talk through whatever crazy idea I came up with and once you got your head around it you'd support it. And I know you would want me to do what's best for me. You wouldn't want me to carry this load on my own without you.

So babe, we're moving.

9th November 2023

I am back trawling through photos and I find one from about six years ago in L.A. at that upmarket Mexican restaurant Red O in Beverly Hills. We look young and full of life. I love this photo of us. We ate some amazing food that trip and got into some funny situations and it's these memories I hold tight.

Because yesterday was another day of drowning. I am sick with a chest infection which isn't helping how I am feeling so I am nauseous and tired and generally feeling off. And then I woke up angry. At you for dying, at you for leaving me, at myself for feeling so miserable and out of control. I never expected loving and then losing you to be so hard. It really feels like I take two steps forward and then three steps back. It feels like it's getting harder. In the grief support group I've joined I can see similarities that others are going through and it makes me feel like I am not losing my mind.

The anger was short-lived and I started on the next task on the never-ending to-do list. And that's when those backward steps showed up with a vengeance and the floodgates opened and the tears flowed for what felt like no reason. But of course that reason is the emptiness that you've left behind.

I can take some comfort knowing that if the patterns are correct, I'll take more steps forward today, I'll recharge my mind, body and soul once again.

As someone said to me, the grief matches the love.

You are loved.

13th November 2023

It's the middle of the night in Paris, France right now and it's not so much a memory today but 'what would have been' in my imagination. We would be tucked up sound asleep in our boutique hotel right now in Paris. We would have been out exploring the city the last couple of days in our new warm clothes we would have bought along the way as the weather turned cold in that part of the world. We would have dressed up and been to Moulin Rouge and you would have asked me to iron your shirt and I would have grumbled and asked if you were going to definitely wear that one because the last time I ironed your shirt you wore a different one, and you would have laughed at me.

Sending Up the Flare

We would have found some new restaurants to eat at amongst all the sights the city has to offer. And we would have already packed our bags ready to head off to the airport in the morning for our journey home. We would have laughed at the packing process as you looked at how on earth you were going to fit everything into your suitcase and you would ask me to help, aka me do your packing for you, as you looked on just like our last night in Morocco.

We may or may not have been ready to leave this journey and get home, but that's one thing we'll never know.

Instead I've been packing boxes and the moving container doing my best Tetris, pushing things into gaps that no one can see, for the next part of my life's journey without your physical presence. I can feel you looking on, keeping watch over it all and maybe a little frustrated that you're a silent observer instead of being in amongst it all.

In my mind, in a few more hours that plane we were booked on will leave Charles De Gaulle airport without us.

What would have been.

15th November 2023

Babe, it's been 4 weeks, 2 hours and 35 minutes since I turned the bedside light on and turned to face you but your heart had already stopped beating. That is the hardest thing I've ever had to face in my life. My world fell apart in that moment and my heart and soul shattered in little pieces.

Spousal Grief

Whilst I continue to move forward, as time does not stand still, I can't help but continue to look back at the same time. As I pour through photos of our life together urgently trying to find more pictures with you in them, I realise how I must be truly grateful for the life we did have together, the life we created on our terms.

It has taken this long for me to fully grasp that you are not coming back. And boy do I feel shortchanged about that.

I keep thinking about when we met, how we talked for hours and the venue closed around us finally asking us to leave so they could go home. We were two people looking for a connection. We wanted someone to love who would love us in return. We found that connection that night and decided we were prepared to give it our best shot.

Thank you Ryan, for loving me the best you knew how. We created a great life together and had many adventures right until that moment in time. I am glad I was able to give you the love you deserved.

Chapter 3

Grief Is the Shadow of Love

16th November 2023

I joined a widow and widowers support group today. I really need the warm and precious safe space to vent, to yell, to cry, to laugh and one day to show support to others as they join the same group and go through the same nightmare.

I told them about your death, our dream holiday, how it was to be our last full day in Portugal before flying to Madrid. We had so many plans and dreams.

I told them I am arranging your memorial with my beautiful support group around me. That your mother is proving to be very challenging and I am struggling with her making it all about her instead of honouring you on your terms and wishes. I understand she is hurting and I don't want to hurt her in return so I am biting my tongue. I told them you didn't have the best relationship with her. As if losing you wasn't enough, I've got to deal with the condescension again without you being here to buffer it. I hear of others' stories about their struggles with their loved ones families and how they coped. I hear of stories where they have so much love and support from their spouse's family but their own family are not stepping up. And there are the stories with variations of both. The one thing that stands out with this group is the safety of sharing your deepest thoughts with others who know and won't judge you for it.

22nd November 2023

Babe I needed you today Ryan. I've had the longest day and didn't realise just how fragile I still am. My anxiety is still through the roof. It's been five weeks today since you've been gone and today I needed you desperately.

Our furbaby Jasper is sick. I started the day at the vet and was so sure I was going to lose him next. I totally broke down at the vet and every fear came tumbling out. And all I wanted was you beside me to talk it all through, for us to support each other through those fears and unknowns. His heart murmur has escalated so quickly in three months and the greatest fear was he was in heart failure. He spent the day at the vet and then at the end of the day they wanted me to go to Emergency. I rang around and jumped in the car for a mad dash up to Brisbane for another opinion. Tonight he's back home with me and things are looking a bit more positive.

Then I get into bed and check messages and your sister has decided I haven't answered her questions well enough, and that she's been 'very patient and polite'!! I am done. The sense of entitlement is astounding. And to point out that the eight years I knew you for wasn't the same as their 51 years was just cruel. Her and your mother will not accept that I am having a memorial the way YOU wanted, not what they or even I might think is nice. I will honour you and your wishes. End of story. It's not a discussion.

It's going to be a very casual thing in line with your specific wishes as we had both discussed what we wanted if the other died first. I didn't expect you to pass at 51 years old but I must honour you. You trusted me with this. You knew, you warned me that I would have to be firm with them if you passed first. They won't leave me alone to do what you wanted. They keep pushing for what they want. They can't understand, or won't accept, that they're a guest on the day. You always told me you hated the circus they created in their lives and told me, 'Do not let them turn my time into a circus'.

I've been nice, I've been firm, I've even ignored them as my anxiety rises. But I've had enough. I will never see them again after this anyway. It was always inevitable. After your mother's bitter outburst earlier in the year, you coming to my defence and nearly throwing her out, it was always a foregone conclusion that I would cut all ties then with your blessing. And you were prepared to never see her again in this lifetime. Yet here we are. Their story is not mine to tell but how it affects me is mine to feel.

Today I really needed you.

25th November 2023

You have such a beautiful smile Ryan. I am looking at a photo of us staying up on the mountain that my work gifted us on my early retirement. We had such a magical time being totally spoilt in our own cabin in amongst the rainforest, massages, spa bath, bubbly and beer, amazing food and quality time together.

As I revisit this beautiful memory I am brought back to earth with a thud. We will never experience this again together, that's the cold hard truth.

And I recognise my reality these past few days has me seeing a comedian on TV and laughing out loud then hearing you laughing with me, only to realise that it's only my imagination.

It has me reading an advertisement and thinking I must remember to tell you about that new product when you get home, but you're not coming home.

It has me making a pot of soup, tasting it and hearing you say, 'That's really good babe' and I put aside enough for you for lunch tomorrow. But there are no more tomorrows for you.

Grief Is the Shadow of Love

I forget for just a moment that you're gone and just as quickly I remember. And I know that you're the only person I want to tell these things to. I just want to talk to you!!

But life is not always fair and so I continue on my way, focusing on reliving that beautiful memory of our time in our secluded cabin in the rainforest.

27th November 2023

You and I together forever babe.

We had a memorial for you today. So many wonderful people came to show their love and respect for YOU. Sadly, it was marred by your sister intimidating and threatening me. You warned me and I knew there would be some hostility but I didn't expect the vicious, in-my-face confrontation. Your sister threatened me with court over your ashes. My family and friends were shocked by her venomous display and it rattled me in my vulnerable state. I asked her not to do this now and said that if she continues then she should leave. I ended up in tears sitting out in the lounge of the club trying to pull myself together.

It was a no-brainer for you that your remains would stay with me. We had a life together, I am your partner and next of kin. After the way you were treated by your previous partner's family when she passed, you never wanted me to feel the way you felt if you passed first. You thought it was a cool idea to have ashes being in jewellery and you said if I wanted that then I could wear some of your ashes, but that the rest should remain together with me. So I wear you in a gold heart around my neck. I will always honour your wishes as we discussed and not let anyone take that from you.

Your father was a true gentleman. He spoke of how you had lost touch with your family for many many years, making your way alone in life. And then you met me. He said the last eight years of your life where we were together were the best eight years of your whole life, a sentiment I have heard repeatedly since you passed.

My family and some of Jet's friends came back to our house afterwards and we all had a few drinks. Discussion centred initially around the threats and my sister-in-law was shocked as she had missed that encounter. I know how angry you would have been witnessing that and I would not have wanted to be on the receiving end of your wrath. You are not here to defend your wishes or defend me, but I feel your support of removing her from my life completely.

I love you forever Ryan. I still cannot fully grasp that you can be gone so quickly from my life.

28th November 2023

This is my tribute to you, Ryan, from your celebration of life yesterday. My heartfelt thanks to Dean, our friend and Celebrant, for reading this out to those gathered in support. You know my emotions take over and I am not capable of speaking during times of such distress.

Grief Is the Shadow of Love

'Love shouldn't be complicated. Ryan was not a complicated man. He just wanted me to love him, warts and all. Simple.

It's not the amount of time you know someone, it's the quality of that time together that counts. Ryan and I had 7 years and 10 months physically together and we crammed a lifetime into that time we had. We enjoyed being together, doing things together, supporting each other, travelling the world together. Reminiscing over all of our photos showed me just how much we did as one, how joined at the hip we were, how blessed I was to be able to share life with him.

And he showed support of my vegan lifestyle from the moment we met. He never ridiculed me or made me feel like it was a drama, he enjoyed how it opened his mind and his heart to so many things in the world that he never considered before. There were definitely times I pushed him outside his comfort zone, and I am so glad I did or he never would have had the chance to show the world what he was truly capable of, the huge capacity for caring he had and the charity work he got involved in and supported.

Ryan always wanted the best for everyone and my boys were at the top of that list. From day one he wanted to support me as a single mother to teenagers. He always told me that everything he did was to try to take any stress away from me and see me happy.

Ryan is the reason we have Devon Rex cats. And he took to the role of foster cat dad to all the babies we took in effortlessly. He loved every little soul who came through our home and they loved him too. You can tell a man's character by the way they treat animals.

Spousal Grief

On our recent travels we rescued a very sick little kitten from the streets who now lives a happy and healthy life at an English language school in Fes in Morocco. We sat in on some classes with the students and met their families and the wider community during our stay and we were welcomed with open arms. I could see how the young men admired Ryan, and upon news of his passing the impact he had on them was obvious through their outpouring of messages of support, lighting of candles and prayers, their families' concern for me and their overall sadness. He left his mark.

Ryan is so much more than the labels placed upon him; a chef, a surfer, a jokester, a Devon lover, a foster cat dad, a stepdad and many others.

There's so much I could tell you about Ryan. But in the end for me the only important thing is I got to love him and I was lucky to receive his love in return.'

30th November 2023

Today I am looking at a picture of you in our Airbnb. Not sure how I feel about this photo to be honest babe. This is our apartment in Porto and it was taken just after we arrived. Your surprised look does make me laugh because you were a man who loved pulling faces but it's bittersweet at the same time knowing what happened in that space behind you just three days later.

Grief Is the Shadow of Love

We had such shitty weather the whole time we were there. You really wanted to get to the ocean even though it wasn't surfing weather, but you never made it that final day.

So I've now found a project that I know you would have absolutely loved the concept of. It's called One Last Wave. They memorialise people's loved ones (that's you) by carefully etching their names onto surfboards that are hand-shaped locally and then carry them out into the ocean to catch a symbolic one last wave as an active way to honour them in the one place they really loved being, the ocean.

So babe, your name will be honoured and memorialised on their 7th board that will be launched in the beautiful healing waves of Cornwall, United Kingdom in another new part of the world you've never surfed. It can take a few months to be completed. It's another way to deeply respect you and your love of surfing, keep you travelling the world and it's a memorial that doesn't take away from your final wishes. As a project, it is in total alignment with your views in this world.

Anyone wanting to follow the process can do so through their social channels on Instagram (@onelastwaveproject), Twitter (@onelastwave), and Facebook (@onelastwaveproject) with information about the board's release as well as videos and images to see once it is completed.

5th December 2023

What a week last week was babe! I know you have faith in me being able to deal with whatever is thrown at me but enough is

Spousal Grief

enough. On top of everything that's happened since you passed, on Friday the Hilux was stolen and the idiot who took it left his old beat-up piece of s$&t in its place in our driveway …. yes seriously!!

Well, I am relying on you to use whatever spiritual powers you've got now and put them to good use, a forcefield of positive good vibes only around us for the future is in order.

So in that positive vein I settle on a photo that is a beautiful reminder of what we were creating coming together as a couple all those years ago on our first 'family' overseas trip. You'd never been to Bali and we were very happy to show you parts of the island we know so well, enabling you to visit and surf the spots you had always wanted to.

But what made this trip extra special is one particular thing you said to me. We had all jumped on a boat for a day trip to Nusa Lembongan and had a great day, with you and Max surfing, us all swimming, the boys stand-up paddle boarding and as we sat on the beach having a drink at the end of the day waiting for the boat to take us back, you turned to me and with such joy on your face you said, 'I can't remember ever feeling so happy in my life, being here with you is the best feeling I've ever had'. I've never forgotten that moment and I never will. I've carried it in my heart all this time as it took up residence immediately and never left.

So many great moments we've had since but that one short sentence has to be right up in the top three wonderful memories that I can recall at a moment's notice. I am so happy that you got to feel that way in your life, it's something everyone deserves at least once in a lifetime.

Grief Is the Shadow of Love

10th December 2023

Only four sleeps to go babe until we move house. You'd be proud of the way so many have stepped up and selflessly helped get the property up to scratch ready for sale. We are truly surrounded by amazing people and thank you doesn't seem enough.

I've been busy with so many things to finalise so it's kept my mind distracted, but of course the nights are always the hardest, the empty house, the empty bed, the silence. I've slept on your side since returning home, but it gives me little comfort.

The thing is there is no moving on, no getting through 'this'. There is only moving forward as best I can because I am still alive and that's what living is all about.

I've learnt grief just creeps up on you.

Grief taps you on the shoulder whenever it wants.
Grief does not care for manners and appearances.
Grief must be heard when it wants to be.
And I am learning that is perfectly ok.

Yesterday I was driving home from the shop, all very mundane, and suddenly grief decided to tap me on the shoulder and take me right back to the moment I lost you. I could feel the room, the way you looked, how I didn't get enough time with you before they came to take you away. And so so much more.

Bam. It was so intense and I sobbed all the way home.

Spousal Grief

That's what grief does. Just when I thought the heartwrenching sobbing was getting further apart, it comes back with a vengeance in the midst of doing something very normal.

I had made a conscious decision this week that I need to spend better time on my grief, on my healing and do some things that I find comfort and enlightenment doing. The beach walks and grounding are definitely helping but I need more than that.

So …
Today I went to a new sound healing. I was so looking forward to it and then I became emotional and spent the first half hour crying. I had this excruciating pain in my shoulder blade, babe you know where I hold my emotions, and then you came through so clearly with my pop in tow. The physical pain was so intense I thought I was having a heart attack. I really thought I was going to have to get up and leave. You watched me so intently that for a while I thought you were just observing me in my pain and I was angry with you, but then you smiled the brightest smile all the while holding my gaze and not letting it go and you told me, 'It's all ok'. And the pain disappeared just like that with those three words you said to me … it's all ok. And I realised you weren't observing me, you were so focused on drawing my pain of losing you away. I felt so much love from you, the crying stopped and for the remaining hour I was deeply at peace.

Thank you for showing up for me today babe. I think I'll sleep well tonight.

Grief Is the Shadow of Love

13th December 2023

Eight weeks ago we were sitting at dinner and we had no idea it was to be your last meal on this earth, that it was to be our last meal together.

I know it was raining outside, I know we wore matching raincoats to walk up the road, I know it was the best food we'd had on this trip, I know the space was beautiful in my favourite colour, I know the waiter was a really lovely Brazilian man with a boundless knowledge of Portuguese wines, I know we talked about our future plans, I know we had deep meaningful conversation, I know it was a magical evening.

But I can't remember anything really clearly, it is all muted. There's a lot of important stuff missing, just like in the last photo I have of that night.

I can only remember your last breath less than 12 hours later. I can clearly recall that next morning, every single detail.

So I wake up this morning with a wet pillow, swollen eyes, a snotty nose and tears on my cheeks.

I want to talk to you. I want to go for a walk in a new city with you. I want to hold your hand. I want to plan our day together. I want to hear your voice. I really want to hold your hand. I want you to make it all better.

I am reminded how humans measure time and the cycle of that measurement throughout our lives.

Spousal Grief

When we are born we start with days, weeks and months in those first two years of life. Then we move on to years and fractions of years, as young children we are six-and-a-half or nearly nine. As we reach mid-teens we are desperate to be older so we sometimes lie about being 18. By the time we are heading towards those 40 and 50 milestones we revert back a little to lying but it's about being younger. We are scared of aging. And when we are elderly it changes again, if we are lucky enough to get into our 90s we cherish every moment of time and start talking with pride in fractions again, 93 and a half, nearly 95, will be 97 next birthday.

Then comes the death of a loved one. And we go back to counting in days, weeks and months again. And that is where I find myself, counting each day and week since you've been gone. But there is no joy in this measurement of time.

You don't lose someone once, you lose them over and over again, every single day. Knowing this is part of life does not make it any easier.

So babe, eight weeks since we said our last cheers together. I will cherish that.

Chapter 4

The Weight of New Beginnings

14th December 2023

After a huge day moving I am finally putting my feet up and having a quiet scotch. The bed is made, two of the cats are settled, two are not happy, and Emma our senior dog is slowly getting used to being in a new space. Such a hot day and I eventually found some swimmers so jumped in the pool for a refreshing cool off and I am scrounging up something to eat, probably cereal as I ate everything else before I moved!!

I have found I have a jackfruit tree in the yard with two huge fruits so I am happy to find that after leaving our pomegranate and mango trees both prolifically producing.

Spousal Grief

I have worked out the internet, the TV (on the floor) and found the remote control. I call that a massive achievement as that is normally your domain. I may have upended your tub of cables. Not sure where the phone charger is though.

Tomorrow I'll open some more boxes and continue nesting in my new home.

18th December 2023

Happy anniversary babe. Today would have been eight years together.

Last night one of our beautiful friends asked how we met and I realised that I get asked that a lot. And I then appreciate that we know our story because it's ours but we assume everyone else knows it too.

So I reflect on how we met online and then on our first in-person meeting and it always makes me laugh.

Through the online dating app we had only exchanged a couple of messages and then you went a bit silent. I was a bit over the online thing as there are so many non-genuine people on there and I was ready to give it all up and remain single. So in my normal straightforward fashion I messaged you saying, 'Are you interested or not, it's fine either way, just be up front and say so, don't do the ghost thing and let's not waste each other's time'.

The Weight of New Beginnings

You responded a day or so later and apologised profusely, telling me you were in Hawaii and your phone had caught on fire and you had to get a new phone and sort things out. Well you can imagine my thoughts on that BS response. What a wanker, just another idiot with some tall story to tell that I would never hear from again. You then sent me your phone number and said you would be back in Australia in a few days. This triggered Big Brother and social media to put your profile on my FB feed of 'people I might know'. I still thought you were full of shit. But my curiosity got the better of me and I had a quick look at your page and out of the very few posts you made there was one telling all your friends about your phone mishap and why you hadn't responded to anyone. Hmmm, maybe you weren't such a bad guy after all.

After you got back home you asked me out for a drink and we met at the surf club. It was mid-week and I got there and sat in my car and thought I could not really be bothered. Online dating can be very draining and extremely disappointing. I thought that maybe I'd just go home and send you a message saying sorry something came up and I couldn't make it. Then you walked past the front of my car and I thought I think that's him. Yeah, doesn't look like his profile picture, typical he's put up a younger photo. I was more determined to just leave but my manners got the better of me so I thought just one drink and I'll politely exit the building.

We sat with that one drink and talked for hours until the club shut around us and asked us to leave as they were closing. We just had so much to say to each other and it was so easy and natural.

Spousal Grief

Over the years that followed we would laugh about the start of our love story. You would say you were lucky that I was persistent and sent that message asking straight up for clarity otherwise you would have assumed I wasn't interested and moved on, and in turn I would have closed down my profile.

We may have been very different people that night but we somehow just fit like a jigsaw puzzle from that very first meeting. And we decided then and there that we would wake up each day and give it our best shot at seeing if we could have a lasting relationship. We were meant to be and I am grateful we got to create a life together. I am also grateful I was there with you at the end of your time on earth.

Your beautiful friend Di told me how she was talking to your mother at your memorial and said you were always so lost and sad for a long time until we met and that I was the best soul for you, and your mother agreed. She also told me that after that first drink of ours you rang her and told her that you 'met this chick and she was 'the one''. I remember you saying, 'You look just like your profile picture,' and I said, 'Well that's because it's current' and we laughed. She also said you weren't clear on exactly what I did for a living but thought I was a secretary and you wanted to get a better job to look after me and my kids. She said you were just a nice guy looking for your place in the world and you found it with me. How lucky was I?

Today's date means so much to me as it is linked to so many things in my life. I moved to Queensland, it would have been our anniversary and it is the birthday of a special person for a family member who never saw her 21st birthday.

The Weight of New Beginnings

So I am raising a glass of Portuguese wine to represent your passing in Portugal, drinking out of my mother's wine glass who passed six months after moving to this state, nibbling on pickled onions which were the favourite snack of my father, who made the interstate move possible, eating olives which I found a love for on our recent trip to Italy and including Ellie in my thoughts to support my niece on this day.

Cheers to the ones we love and lost.

19th December 2023

Five years ago today we had our friends and family opening for our restaurant. We certainly did a lot together. I recall cooking for our favourite feline charity fundraiser when a friend was visiting us. She commented saying that to watch us in the kitchen together was something else. The whole mood in the house changed from laidback, pottering around to an electric atmosphere of purpose. We were totally in sync with each other, we worked together like an orchestra knowing all our parts without having to speak, it was poetry in motion. We definitely complemented each other when we cooked together and the result was food full of love. I feel it was reflective of us as a couple – we fit together like guacamole and corn chips haha.

Spousal Grief

23rd December 2023

I saw this today and it made so much sense to me.

Holiday host etiquette: If you're inviting someone to your home and they're grieving, be sure you're inviting their grief to attend, too. It will be there, anyway.

Don't invite someone with the goal of cheering them up for the holidays. Don't expect them to put on a happy face in your home. Don't demand they fake it 'til they make it or do something they don't want to do, either.

Invite them with the loving intention of offering cheer and companionship and unconditional care during the holidays. To do this, you will need to honour and be responsive to their needs and emotions.

You can do this by privately acknowledging their grief when you make the invitation:

'I know this season is extra hard and your heart is hurting. You and your grief are welcome in our home. Come as you are, we'd be honoured to have you with us.'

It's also incredibly loving to honour the reality that it's often hard for grieving folks to know what they will want, need, be up for, or able to tolerate at the holidays. Giving them an invite without the need for commitment and permission to change their mind is extra loving:

The Weight of New Beginnings

'You don't have to decide right now. If it feels good to be with us, we will have plenty of food and love for you – just show up! I'll check in again the day before to see if you're feeling up to coming over and if there's anything you'd like me to know about how we can support you.'

Your grieving friends and fam need attentive care and responsiveness at the holidays, not plans to keep them busy, distracted, and happy.

If they're laughing, laugh with them.

If they're weeping, ask if they'd like your company or your help finding a quiet place to snuggle up alone for a while.

If they're laughing while weeping, and this is more common than you'd think, stay with them – this is a precious moment of the human experience that is truly sacred.

We don't need to protect ourselves or each other from grief at the holidays. In fact, the more we embrace grief as an honored holiday guest, the more healthy, happy, and whole our holidays will be.

Sarah Nannen

These are very wise words.

I have also worked out that it is not my job to make others feel comfortable in my grief, my responsibility is to me and me alone.

Spousal Grief

25th December 2023

Day 69.

Another emotionally charged milestone. It feels like I am in a holding pattern that never ends and I cannot ever see it changing.

Today is another day just like all the others in the last couple of weeks. I wake up early and I am surprised yet again that you are not here. I have generally migrated to your side of the bed because there's no resistance of course. I shed some tears and get up.

Emma needs to go out to the toilet, Mila and Zima are in position ready for their breakfast. Jasper will leave the warmth of our bed at the last minute and Murray pretends he's not starving and will only pop his head up as he hears the food bowls being put down.

All of this happens through blurred vision as my eyes are filled and my cheeks are wet. And then I get on with the rest of my day.

Jet and Charlee arrived and gave me a framed picture of you and I and I cried.

The rest of our little family will be here soon and this year everyone is contributing to our midday meal. It is not you and I cooking together, working together as the well-oiled team we are. But I know you will be standing in spirit at my right shoulder, your new place in my world, observing what's going on and sticking your finger in what I am making, pinching a taste and smiling and asking if I was following a recipe or 'wing-ding-a-linging' it as you laugh because you know me so well.

The Weight of New Beginnings

I am making Aperol Spritz to sip on today in memory of our magical time in Italy earlier this year

I do wonder for a split second what gift we would have decided on for ourselves. It would definitely have involved travel. Maybe it was going to be our plans for Tasmania in February or a month in Vietnam. Or possibly even a quick getaway to Bali to re-live our earliest trip together. What I do know is I will continue to travel, solo again, knowing you would want me to live our dreams and not let them die with you.

Last night I found an old television news clip of you being interviewed on the opening of the Mexican Kitchen at The Collective and I replayed it over and over just to hear you speak those few brief words. Even though I have always loved my quiet time to disengage from the excessive noise in the world, I really miss hearing your voice, your unique way of calling out hello as you walked in the door. The silence is deafening!

I kept it together the rest of the day but found I just didn't have much to say about anything. I smiled and laughed and chatted but I felt disconnected and as though I was just going through the motions.

Once everyone left I fed the animals, poured a glass of wine, lit a candle for you and sobbed. I think I just needed to decompress from this first of many Christmases to come.

So Merry Christmas babe.

Chapter 5

A World Without You

<u>1st January 2024</u>

I can't believe it's a new year babe. It makes me feel sick in my stomach to be honest. 2023 I lost you and now it is 2024. It just makes it sound so long ago when in fact it is only ten weeks and five days since you passed and there is not a day that goes by that I don't wish I could turn back time.

I can literally smell, feel, hear and taste Portugal and our time there, I just can't touch your physical presence. And that makes me feel profoundly sad, it is an emotion that lives with me daily.

I've been surrounded by family and friends who I love and they love me but the truth is I am still alone and lonely even in a crowded room. I am still going to bed and waking up alone each day.

Spousal Grief

I miss the simple act of us going out to dinner together. We would generally decide last minute that neither of us felt like cooking and one of us would ring our restaurant of choice and make a last-minute booking. We didn't need to have a special occasion or reason, we didn't need to get all dressed up, we were just happy to be together doing our thing. I need to find a way of doing that simple act of just going out and sitting at a restaurant for a last-minute meal … alone.

One big positive distraction has taken place though Ryan, and that is I am fostering kittens again. The call went out to collect some abandoned babies at Animal Emergency at Underwood. I had forgotten how much joy the foster babies bring to me, and my heart is full of love for these gorgeous darlings. The three grey siblings are absolutely divine but it is my little four-week-old ginger baby that I really think has been placed in my way for a reason to help me. He reminds me so much of our gorgeous Moroccan rescue kitten baby Cimba and I am so in love with him. I even sent photos to Driss in Morocco to show him the uncanny resemblance and he was so surprised by this little twin. I've called him Aris and he has given me a reason to get up each morning – to give him the love and care that he so deserves. He thinks I am his mumma running to greet me with tiny meows every time he sees me. He climbs onto my lap and falls asleep close to my heart. I love them all of course but this little guy is very special.

As this first day of the new year draws to a close I am feeling quite emotional as I miss you immensely. I can't really put into words what I am feeling. I thought I had myself together pretty well this week but my newest friend grief wants time in the limelight yet again and gives me no choice in the matter.

2023 gave us so many special times, so many amazing experiences and memories I'll carry forever babe. It also gave me the single hardest moment in my life so far.

I can only wonder what 2024 has in store.

6th January 2024

Big achievement today. I have sorted your tangled box of cables. It seems rather pitiful that I call this an achievement, but sometimes the energy to complete such a simple task is all-consuming and I have to celebrate that I got it done. I cannot for the life of me think why I need any of these leads, Ryan, I am open to insight from the other side babe. If it's not forthcoming they will all be going down to the tip recycling centre. What are the odds that as soon as I let them go I will need one of them? I am willing to roll the dice on that one.

7th January 2024

I have an overwhelming feeling of wanting to go away somewhere, anywhere, where nobody knows me, nobody knows you are gone. Then those strangers I may talk to don't ignore that you're gone because they never knew you existed. They think I am a solo traveller passing through living life, travelling the world. I think I would rather be lonely in the presence of strangers than in the presence of those who know you died eleven-and-a-half weeks ago but seem to have forgotten you already.

Spousal Grief

I am struggling tonight.

Off to bed to try to sleep.

14th January 2024

Another extremely busy week done which really just means another week without you babe. There is not a day that goes by where I feel not only your physical absence but I am miserably aware how much of a team we were. I spent most of my life being very independent, very capable, doing everything for myself and then you came along and you so easily became the one person who I could rely on, who became my other half, who was there when I woke each morning and the last one I saw when I closed my eyes each night. And I am dismally reminded of this each and every day.

I am tired after the hectic week gone by but it is a good tired. Today Josh and Jet helped me go through what was left in the garage at the old house, we have a pile for the tip and a pile to keep and will get it finished this week. I have achieved some things I needed to accomplish and I will sleep well and be ready to hit the ground running to meet the demands in place for another jam-packed week ahead.

I had a couple of missed calls during the day of busy activity and when I finally got to them they were from your mother. Seeing her name causes unease, listening to the condescending tone gives me anxiety and the demands that I must drive to see her as she is on the coast make me shut down completely. I am not strong enough to filter her insincerity and I am not entertaining the toxic mind games she plays. So I decide that I will not return her calls of demand.

As I keep being told by grief support, healing support and self-care practices, it is ok to say no, my yeses are sacred and not something to be given lightly. So my days and weeks take this into account in every decision I make for my emotional and physical well-being during the biggest heartbreak I have ever faced.

Grief has become my friend, something not to be feared or avoided. She is welcome at my table whenever I need to hear from her. She is a form of self-care. And I now know it is possible to grieve and move forward at the same time.

It is so easy to remember you Ryan, I do it every day without any effort. It is also very easy to miss you as I do that daily too. When the missing you gets overwhelming and it seems nearly everyone else has forgotten I just remind myself that I knew you best, I love you most and I will always feel your absence the greatest. That is what choosing each other every day means.

15th January 2024

I went for a beach walk first up and let the calming of the sights and sounds of the ocean wash over me. Breathing in the good shit and breathing out the bullshit works in this beautiful place. I think of you when I look at the surfers in the water, all of them ready to catch the perfect wave. My phone rang during my walk and it was your mother again. I felt the familiar knot in my stomach at her name and took a deep breath to let it slide off me. I refuse to let it upset my time of self-care this morning.

Then this afternoon she sends me a message which starts 'Kiely'!! Really!! She now cannot spell my name. It says it all really. This simple act is not a mistake. It immediately puts me on the defensive. She is demanding me to answer more questions about your 'sudden death' and wants to see the coroner's report, which she knows I do not have yet. Along with other things, the message upsets me. I react. I also keep my response calm but need to set clear boundaries. I explain I have been very busy and have a lot on my plate. I explain again I have no report to show her and that they released your body as there was nothing out of the ordinary. I briefly outlined again what happened on the morning you died and tell her I have no desire to rehash your death over and over again with her, it was very traumatic for me to 'watch the man I love suddenly die beside me with no warning and I already re-live it daily' and 'my grief counselling is guiding me through it'. I signed it off KYLIE as I am still pissed she did that to my name.

Boundary set, I have no desire to speak to her again and she must respect that her final outburst at our home last year will not be forgotten. She cannot take back what she said and how she feels. I get to choose who is in my life and it is not her, something you gave your blessing to me on when you were alive.

16th January 2024

Looks like Jasper approves of our choices babe. I've finally unpacked the Moroccan rugs, one you chose and one I chose and he is rolling around on them, making them his own. Not sure where they are going in this house as we chose them for the other house but I am sure I will work it out. We both fell in love with the architecture and design over there and I will be able to bring that in with changes I make in future in this new home.

The Berber man who handled the sale and one of the widows who makes these by hand were beautiful people. He understood I did not want to look at wool or hair and put them away to only show me cactus fibre rugs. And once he knew I respected all life he offered you 500,000 + camels for me being vegan and another 500,000 + for me being a good negotiator, two attractive qualities in a wife apparently. We did have a laugh about it and discussed how many Aussies do not have such kind views of vegans and are quite negatively triggered simply by the term. The Berber widow, in contrast, hugged me and kissed my arms once she understood what vegan translated to and found out about our foster furbabies too. She said we will be favoured when we die.

The old man also spent time teaching me some basic Arabic so we could communicate more effectively with the local people of Morocco. It certainly enhanced our experience and cemented our love for such beautiful people. And you got a kick out of watching me talk and be understood.

So as life certainly still goes on for me with you gone, I will treasure our experiences, our choices on our travels and will have permanent reminders of the fun we shared in those moments.

Shukran Ryan, we had fun in Morocco and I will return there one day to visit the lifelong friends we made.

Spousal Grief

17th January 2024

Up early today to meet the young man labouring for me at the old house cleaning up the gardens so the house can finally be put on the market for sale. Fairly uneventful day really, which is nice to be able to breathe and rest the nervous system a little.

Spoke far too early though didn't I. At 6.35pm there is a text message on my phone from your mother. She has decided she cannot hold her tongue any longer and gives it to me in true-to-form fashion. Takes me back to her verbal tirade at our home in April last year. She tells me that she finds me sharing my grief 'quite bizarre and emotionally draining for her'. That is really very cruel and I actually lost my breath reading those words. I am sympathetic to your mother as a mother losing her son but I cannot give her the forgiveness she wants from you for her nasty behaviour, it is not my job to lie to her and say you told me you forgave her because you didn't tell me that. At the same time, I won't remind her of your anger with her back then as there is no point punishing the woman. She goes on to say she could block me 'of course' but needs to keep a record for the counselling she too is having. She calls me disrespectful, that your sister and I clashed at your memorial (I am not sure how open intimidating threats equals a clash of opinion), and that I am clearly unaware of how much your parents loved you. I can only sit back and laugh because otherwise I would cry or worse. Thankfully, I am very aware that your mother has one perspective of life only and that is her own and as I told you over the years, I am not offended by that.

I think back to the only time in our nearly eight years together that you felt compelled to protect me against an attack by another person, your mother. I am reminded that in that moment I felt even more loved by you, a man of few words when it comes to anything emotional. But as you told a number of our friends, you 'will not have anyone speak to Kylie like that, it doesn't matter who they are'. That distasteful encounter brought us even closer together.

The decision is made. I am well and truly done.

I press the block button for her.

24th January 2024

I had a massage today.

It has been 14 weeks since you died.

One of so many things I miss is some form of physical contact, some form of touch. Humans need that. The hugs we get from family and friends never last long enough. So I have found that having a regular massage gives me a form of physical touch. The skin-to-skin from their hands and arms as the therapist works through the knots and stresses and tension in my back and shoulders, my feet and hands, from my grief, my new norm, helps me immensely for that hour in time.

It is not you, it will never be you again, but it will do for now.

Spousal Grief

26th January 2024

Eight years ago was our first public holiday together with the kids and we went road-tripping with my boys down south. We packed food and checked out some beaches and eventually ended up back at the famous Snapper Rocks in Coolangatta for you and Max to surf. We sat on the rocks and watched the sun go down. We have done so much since then but still had so much planned to do.

1st February 2024

Finally!! I unpacked those beautiful Moroccan dishes we chose on our holiday. They have been sitting in a timber box for months and I have avoided even attempting to tear off the cardboard packaging and pry open the timber frame. I can still taste that amazing vegan tagine the chef made specially for us in Casablanca. The vibrant colours, the tantalising aromas and the balance of flavours were just perfect and such a surprise with every bite. We ate so much that night and rolled out of there with full bellies and full hearts. Right now I cannot see myself attempting it without you beside me in the kitchen looking back at the food photos and working out how she made something so delicious with very little advanced warning. For now they have moved as far as the dining table where they will sit as a reminder of your absence.

Chapter 6

Living in the Grip of PTSD

2nd February 2024

Checking my emails and I have received correspondence from the Australian Consulate about your autopsy report. It is now available from the Portuguese authorities and I need to pay for it. It is going to be in Portuguese as well so then I will need it translated.

I feel a bit numb reading that email.

I have had your death certificate translated already so I suppose I expected that part. I am surprised there is a cost for the report itself. Not that it matters. I think I am more shocked the report is ready because they said six to twelve months and it is only fifteen-and-a-half weeks so I was not prepared to receive it yet.

I ring the Consulate here in Australia and talk it through with them, complete the forms and pay the money. They assure me they will ring me prior to sending the report when it is available, to help soften the reality of opening this type of correspondence. I hang up and analyse my feelings. I am both anxious and relieved that this part of the bureaucracy is nearly complete and I will have definitive findings in black and white about your cause of death.

4th February 2024

'One day you will wake up and there won't be any more time to do the things you've always wanted. Do it now.' I am unsure who wrote these words but they resonate with me more than ever.

Fifteen-and-a-half weeks ago this saying came true for you babe, when your karmic journey ended. I am so thankful we were doing things we wanted. There has been a lesson in such a sudden and overwhelming loss that I am slowly coming to grips with. But then again sometimes shit just happens and there is no lesson to be learnt. Right now I cannot even look at our growing list of things that we wanted to do, that we were going to do. But I will re-visit that list at some point in the future and continue ticking things off and adding new things to it.

Until then I will persist getting into bed alone at night, waking each morning to an empty bed and going through the motions of daily life.

7th February 2024

Sixteen weeks today since you passed.

Three weeks since I had to block your family from the ongoing harassment. Then tonight I receive a solicitor's letter on behalf of your mother with my last name misspelled this time, 'not wishing to aggravate my suffering' and requesting information that she already has, which I am under no obligation to provide anyway. She does not respect boundaries, she does not respect your wishes, she does not respect me as your next of kin, she does not respect me as your life partner, she does not respect that I am carrying out your wishes and will not compromise on my promises to you.

Just when I am getting into a routine and feeling like I can face some things I have been putting off, this drags me down again.

When will the nightmare end?

10th February 2024

Good old Facebook memories!! Your love affair with our furbaby girl Zima started seven years ago. That makes her older than I thought. You so desperately wanted another devon rex furchild in your life but knew my stance on 'adopt don't shop' so the only way it was going to happen was if we rescued one. Enter Zima stage right. The white wicked witch. She had been abandoned in a penthouse on the broadwater as a one-year-old with two designer dogs and that experience had left her scarred. We were the perfect place for her to land after her foster carer nursed her back to good health. She misses you, I can see it in her eyes some days. I am doing my best to give her equal time of my brand of calm love and your rough and tumble she valued so much. But I know I will never be able to replicate exactly your crazy neck and chin scratches that made her worship you as you held her in your arms.

14th February 2024

You are definitely not a hopeless romantic babe, and neither am I. But on this first Valentine's Day without you here, I am feeling cheated out of celebrating our love. All I have now are memories, and I can only reminisce over how you cared for me, the little things you did for me that showed me how you loved. You were someone I could rely on, someone I could depend on and that meant so much more than flowers or chocolates. On our last holiday together I needed an ear specialist in Morocco, you took charge, went and found out how you could get help for me and then made it happen. The day before you died you made an appointment for me to see a podiatrist near our Airbnb for the next day because I had mentioned how my ingrown toenail in particular was troubling me with all the walking we were doing. These might seem like small unimportant things but to me they were actions that showed love and care. It was what you did. You just made things happen that I needed, took the hassle away from me and looked out for me in small simple ways. You knew I am a very capable woman but you took charge when I was vulnerable, when you knew I needed it and did it without fuss.

Today I miss that solidness that made up part of the man that was you.

I miss my unromantic Valentine.

22nd February 2024

Eighteen weeks and one day since your last words, your last breath, your last heartbeat Ryan, time truly slips away like the sand in the hourglass.

There is a photo that was taken of you at a brewery in the Yarra Valley years ago. It was the first time you had been to Melbourne and we were going to stay at my BFF's house to go to see Rob Thomas at the winery. Without knowing how much you loved Rob and the history attached to that, Faye had organised for us to meet him as a surprise. You were over the moon. As we stood in the VIP line for our meet and greet you saw me in action for the first time fooling the people behind us into thinking I was one of the musicians ready to go on stage and play tambourine. It took you some time to work out what I was doing, nearly giving me away several times, until I said laughing, 'Can you just roll with me on this one?' At the end of that trip before we left for home, Faye took me aside and said, 'You're perfect for each other'. She knew then what we were still discovering.

Our few trips down south were always to see live music and at the same time each year. I loved seeing the joy within you, seeing my hometown through your eyes. I loved the fun we had as well as the tender moments we shared back then. We

Spousal Grief

should have visited more and bought that holiday apartment we talked about.

Back to the present and the weekend that has just been. We had planned to go together to Tasmania for a week leading up to it then pick up the kids from the airport, meet up with family and see Matchbox 20. Instead, both your physical absence and your spiritual presence were both felt deeply. I had two women stop me on Saturday night as we made our way through the crowd, one lady was quite emotional and I thought I must have known her. But I didn't. This stranger said they had been watching me and our group and the love surrounding us was palpable, they thought it was so beautiful radiating out from us all. I believe it was you shining your light on us that night.

Then on the way home on Tuesday night on the plane, every time I closed my eyes I was taken back to that moment I knew you were gone, it was so vivid, like I was there with you shocked at how the hell this was happening and again I believe you were with me on that plane helping me through the rollercoaster of emotions making sure it didn't spill over until I got home for some privacy. Little did I know that was PTSD adding to the mix of losing you. And oddly enough Jasper slept next to my heart again that night like he did the night I arrived home from Portugal without you.

Eighteen weeks and one day feels like it was just moments ago and a lifetime ago all at once, tonight it is so raw.

1st March 2024

I hate bringing this up with you but it's important for me that it is acknowledged and then put to bed. I officially blocked your sister the other day. You remember that fridge from the restaurant you had put online for sale, I had forgotten it was on your marketplace and to be honest, that fridge wasn't a priority for me to check your listings. Well she found it and then sent me a nasty message accusing me of listing it under your name and threatening me….. 'Don't make me report you'. I laughed out loud at this one. I own the fridge, you put it on marketplace last year, and who the hell is she going to report me to and for what? I am not angry but I am upset again. I am not going to defend myself either from such ridiculous petty accusations. I keep reminding myself of two things. Hurt people hurt people, and I get to choose how I react for my own peace.

10th March 2024

The decision and payment is made. I am off to Europe in May. I have this overwhelming urge to finish what we started in some way. After much debate I've booked a double retreat with a road trip in between with the organisers and another guest who is attending both retreats. The first one will be a week in the South of France. It is surrounding the full moon so lots of healing and support from like-minded women in a safe space. It's not the river cruise that started it all but it's a new journey that will help me get back into the world as a solo traveller. The road trip will take us through the south of France and into Italy to Rome then across to Bari which is where the overnight ferry will take us to Greece for the second retreat that is centred around the new moon, so new beginnings and what the future holds. We had planned Greece this year as part of our gap year so these two retreats and their locations just make sense to me.

I have also got a tiny niggle that has grown into a big plan to take my boys and their girlfriends with me to Italy for two weeks beforehand. I figure the cost of their four economy flights would equal your luxury flight so I am going to bite the bullet and offer it to them. It will also serve as emotional support for me before I continue on to France on my own.

I think they are all going to be very excited and somewhat unbelieving when I tell them. That will be fun.

11th March 2024

The One Last Wave Project board number 7 is finished and online. I played and paused and played and paused the video of the finished board, rapidly scanning all the names of people's loved ones to find yours. Success, you are on the far right-hand side near the centre logo, quite easy to spot after all and perfect timing for your birthday month.

Lots of emotions of course, that is part of my life now; to feel your absence and find ways to keep your memory alive.

It will be just over 22 weeks from your passing when this board goes out on its maiden ride. When reading through the names it is sad to think of so many souls are so loved and so missed by their loved ones but the same applies that they are so loved to have been put forward to have their names included in this amazing project.

Now to wait until the launch of the board in the cold waters of Cornwall.

15th March 2024

A new treatment was in store for me today. I booked a lymphatic drainage massage with a young woman who had been recommended to me. It took me a couple of months to get in and today was the day.

A-mazing.

Upon entering the room, the beautiful therapist said she has already tapped into my energy before I got there and asked permission to continue to do so throughout the treatment. She said I am surrounded by all my angels today, they have all crowded into the small room with us. I felt comfort from this and got a bit emotional.

At the end of the treatment she asked me what yellow roses represented to me. I told her the roses mean nothing but the colour yellow is my safe colour, it represents protection. She said every one of my angels walked over to me as I lay on the bed and placed a yellow rose each on me. She sees the word JOY. She said I have lost all joy and I need to find it again. I should start small and build on it.

Spousal Grief

I left the appointment and sat in the car and pondered the message I received. To me the yellow roses mean you and all my angels will hold me safe, protected and most importantly, supported, as I seek the joy I need. It's an important message to receive.

Later that afternoon the therapist sent me a text message with a photo of a car number plate. She said she thinks the yellow flowers might represent Joy as she received a sign as she left work. There was a car next to hers in the carpark shopping centre and it was personalised in yellow letters – JOY.

So many messages, keep them coming babe.

17th March 2024

I have had such trouble sleeping since losing you. Understandable of course. But I know the toll lack of sleep has on one's health. So nearly five months without you by my side the last three nights I have started wearing the Emirates eye sleep mask. It's such good quality and what a difference it has made. I am not tossing and turning and I am actually sleeping and waking up in the morning somewhat rested. This has also resulted in Zima, your daddy's girl, sleeping right up next to me. It feels nice having a solid little body to lean against even if it is a cat and not you.

Chapter 7

Standing at the Crossroads

<u>**20th March 2024**</u>

Twenty-two weeks today babe. Every week I have at least one new realisation. This week two things have settled heavily on me. Firstly, I lost not only my person but my life before 'that day', my life with my person. And secondly, this first year is all about your death, not your life, and I hate that focus.

But it is inevitable because I feel I am constantly dealing with your death in the practical sense. Not only are you not here physically but there are all the things I have to handle in relation to your death. Some things are done immediately like funerals, memorials, superannuation, insurance, bills, but there's things that don't come up until they come up and when they do, are another reminder of your death.

On Saturday I went to the polling booth for Queensland elections and of course you are still on the register as you died overseas. So not only do I have to contact them again about that, pull out the dreaded death certificate and the translation and lodge that, but now I am going to receive a notice fining you for not voting and I will have to fill that form out and attach all the paperwork and return it.

This is why my body feels so depleted even though I don't do anything physical these days. It is the emotional toll of constantly dealing with your death over and over in so many ways.

I take a lot of naps to recharge.

27th March 2024

Today is your 52nd birthday babe and I am sitting looking at the last photos I have taken of you in that last week of yours on earth.

Today is another of those shitty 'firsts' to endure without you. I have had the first day, week, month without you. I have had the first Christmas, today it is your first birthday, in a few days the first Easter, beyond that my birthday and the list seems so big in this first year. I live in hope that down the track when the firsts are all done it won't be so painful.

Standing at the Crossroads

That big rock of heaviness that sits in the bag I pick up and carry around, the bag I open and peer into and run my hands over the rock with its big jagged edges, those edges that poke painful holes in me to let the tears out; I hope that over time those edges are polished smooth by my hands and the hands of time. That eventually, I can look and remember and experience the seconds and thirds and all that follows without the deep raw pain and see only the love and joy.

Today Ryan it is your 52nd birthday, the first birthday without you.

I feel your physical absence every day.

Forever 51.

1st April 2024

Looking at photos again to re-live memories. It's become my favourite pastime even if it is both comforting and distressing. Time moves in one direction and memories in another.

3rd April 2024

My newest discovery since you've been gone is that my circle of people has shrunk and when I think about it there are probably a number of reasons for this. Some people are just uncomfortable. For some it makes them think of their own mortality and they don't want the reminder, while some see me as a single person that doesn't fit into their world anymore. Others just drift away and move on with their lives. It reminds me of the song lyric, 'But her friends were really his friends, no one stops by to see her much anymore'. But they were my friends, not yours. Go figure. There are so many more reasons, but it's not worth the effort to second guess any of them.

I am quieter now. Of course you are not here for me to talk to so that's natural. My life view has changed too so I find myself removing people on the periphery who I no longer align with for so many reasons, not directly relative to your death but more about my life ahead. As I keep telling myself, my time is sacred and not everyone gets a key to the door. I have always accepted the philosophy that people come into our lives for a reason, a season or a lifetime. That includes me being the rest of your lifetime, but the reality is my lifetime is not over. You were either a reason or season for me, or maybe both.

The most beautiful thing to come about is the support I have received in unexpected places. I don't want to diminish the value I place on the expected support like my family and of course my priceless BFF. I have been given the added gift of deepened friendships from those unexpected places, those precious humans who continue to check in on me regularly, who are physically close by for a shoulder to cry on or an ear to vent to and of course that one person who has promised to send out the cavalry if I don't respond to her daily words of love. Because it is something that I have thought more about in these last few months – if I collapsed at home in bed there is no one next to me to see it, there is no one in the house to find me, it could takes days for someone to check in. It gives me comfort that there is one person here that checks in on me.

Standing at the Crossroads

5th April 2024

So today I did this!! Day procedure at Pindara Hospital for a colonoscopy and gastroscopy as a follow-up to bowel cancer screening for some irregularities in the standard testing. Fortunately it was all clear.

There is always some level of anxiety around these sorts of things but today highlights again the unseen and ongoing toll that losing 'your person' has on the body physically. The doctor and the specialist both agree that my health concerns have stemmed from the stress and trauma of your sudden passing.

The level of stress of both the grief and trauma on the body is astonishing. On top of that is added stress from unsupportive people through the worst time of my life and removing them from my life. To be told in black and white 'your grief is bizarre' among other things, is hurtful and destructive and weighs deeply on the stress levels.

Then there is the ongoing bureaucracy that comes with death. The number of people and departments you have to repeat the same information to that makes you re-live it time and again, people who you know have never suffered any loss at all or they would show much more compassion and streamline their processes to reduce the strain on those grieving.

And so much more, so very much more.

But today the worst thing for me is that you weren't here. I am extremely grateful for the many offers of support to drive me to and from hospital but when it is all said and done no one is you. You are not here waking me up at 4am to drink that last awful pre-op drink, you are not driving me to the hospital, you are not the person I fill out as next of kin (that was a kick in the guts), you are not at home worrying how I am going, you are not picking me up afterwards, you are not settling me into bed with a cup of tea and taking my food order and going out to get the ingredients to cook me a comfort meal, you are not cleaning kitty litter and feeding animals, you are not taking the whole load for the day, you are not checking on me while I sleep it off to make sure I am ok.

Simply, you are not physically here!! And nothing changes that fact!!

So today I did this with my funny little red 'allergy' hat and I survived another day without you, my person, by my side.

18th April 2024

It has been six months since you passed.

Back then I could not imagine how I would get through the first month, let alone six months without your physical presence. Without hearing your voice. Without holding your hand. But here we are.

I miss you.
I miss the me from seven months ago.
I miss us.
I miss the happy us.

Standing at the Crossroads

I miss the exploring us.
I miss the traveling us.
I miss the laughing us.
I miss the planning us.
I miss the couple us.
I miss the us that is gone.
I miss you!

20th April 2024

I am looking at one of my most favourite pictures of our Italian travels in June. It was when I surprised you with business class tickets coming home because 'life's too short' right!! You were so excited and couldn't believe it, as you had never really travelled before we met. And we decided that is how we would live life. Little did we know.

So now as I prepare to retrace most of our steps in Italy in a few weeks and then into France where we never got to as you died before we got there, I've been procrastinating on where to stay for the few days between the kids leaving and my retreat starting.

First world problems hey!!! But I know you get it.

Even though I was the one who organised and planned everything, it struck me this morning that this uncertainty is because I don't have you here to say, 'Babe, what do you think' and light up the iPad and start looking for possibilities!!

That sucks big time.

Spousal Grief

21st April 2024

This time last year we had a few different house guests, some lovely memories and some challenging ones and at the same time we were excitedly getting ready to head off on our next adventure to Dubai and Italy. Now I am readying myself to head back in a couple of weeks to retrace many of our steps in Italy on my way to those healing retreats in France and Greece.

As I sit tonight reflecting on the last 12 months, remembering the amazing things we did and how connected and supportive we were with each other through some challenges outside our control, I am sitting sipping on a saffron tea we purchased in the Souks in Dubai, the only tea that you sampled and said you really liked, as you were not a tea drinker in any way.

So I am focused on our time in Dubai tonight. We learnt a lot about ourselves and the United Arab Emirates and had a really happy time together. The tea is a great reminder of that time and is healing and comforting at the same time.

1st May 2024

I am gutted tonight.

I've just left Animal Emergency Services after making a painful but necessary decision to let Jasper cross the rainbow bridge. I held him in my arms as he took his last breath. Not sure how much more I can take.

Standing at the Crossroads

RIP my darling mummy's boy Jasper.
You told me you've had enough and you want to rest.
You're now safe in your cat dad's arms.
Ryan, look after our boy.

The house is very quiet without Jasper trotting around, getting under my feet, pushing his way onto my lap and yelling at me and the world in general. He is such a very loud, funny, quirky, special boy who only had eyes for me. You used to say no one else gets a look in if I am in the house. Now you get him all to yourself.

Jasper was definitely my soul cat and he has carved out a piece of my heart to take with him on his journey to you.

9th May 2024

It is not lost on me that one year ago today we were sitting at the airport waiting to board our plane to commence, what we didn't realise at the time, was to be our gap year of travel, our year of close connection, our year of us, the year you died.

Tonight I continue our dreams alone with a different focus forced upon me.

As I packed for this trip your absence has been felt, the things I relied on you to deal with versus the things you relied on me to do have come up to give me a bite of reality.

It certainly feels very different tonight as I sit alone waiting for the car that will take me to the airport. I have a sense of

Spousal Grief

excitement of course, travel is an amazing experience, but it is a little subdued, like it is not really happening as you are not here to share it with me.

I have lit my candles like I do every night to honour you babe (and now Jasper too) and had a bit of a chat before blowing them out. Zima is not very happy, she looks a bit on edge, she knows I am leaving her again and has told me she's not impressed.

The hard lesson is that tomorrow is, in fact, not promised.

I am taking the trip.
I am living life.
I am going to find joy again.

Chapter 8

Seeking Sunshine in the Shadows

<u>11th May 2024</u>

I have just arrived at my hotel in Rome after 26+ hours of travelling. The flights were good and I was really calm and relaxed the whole way. Even had a mojito for you babe.

I am at the same hotel we stayed at a year ago, even the Wi-Fi password is the same. The lady at the desk recognised me and asked after my husband. Also asked if I was bringing my boys to visit as I had promised.

All good to that point.

Spousal Grief

Got up to my room and walked in, shut the door and burst into tears with big gulping sobs trying to catch my breath. The memories just hit me like that wave of early grief. I can't believe I feel like I have just lost you all over again, the realisation once more that you are not coming back.

I did not expect this.
I thought I had processed all of that.

It is 10pm, I am pretty tired and emotional so am going to bed. I am glad I have the next 24 hours to decompress before the kids arrive.

13th May 2024

My dad's birthday today. I do wonder if you've made contact with each other in the spirit world. I am sure my mum would have sought you out to talk to you about our life.

My boys and their girlfriends joined me in Rome yesterday and I got to spend Mother's Day with them playing tour guide retracing steps we took twelve months ago. We even had lunch at the same restaurant as last year in the marketplace Campo de' Fiori where history shows public executions were held. I laugh as I remember you and I later walking over the bridge to meet Sharon and Scott at that funny little restaurant with that awful food you all ate.

The last couple of days here I have felt your hand on my shoulder reassuring me, steadying me, letting me know you are always close by never leaving my side. Bittersweet of course but feeling blessed to share this experience with my boys.

Missing you like crazy.

16th May 2024

Yesterday we left Rome and headed up the coast to La Spezia. Today is Tori's birthday and we've spent an amazing day on the water with me playing tour guide again. We stopped at a couple of the Cinque Terre villages and the kids decided Manarola was the spot for lunch before a dip in the freezing Gulf of Genoa. Sitting on the rocks, drinking wine and watching them all having the time of their lives brings me great joy, which is the purpose of this trip, to find joy again.

We were here together a year ago, and it felt right to light another candle for you babe. Then the heavens opened and the rain bucketed down whilst we took shelter with another 20 tourists near the takeaway wine window, so I continued sipping my drink and watching people running for cover all over the waterfront. Once it cleared we joined the line for the return ferry. All was well and then suddenly I felt the familiar feeling in my throat where tears seem to start and had to put my sunglasses on as they just started rolling down my cheeks. It just hits so randomly.

Tonight we went to the amazing and only vegan restaurant in La Spezia. I'd thought to book ahead from Australia as I remembered how quickly they booked out and I wanted to share their delicious food with Tori for her birthday dinner. The same guy was there

Spousal Grief

running bar, taking orders and running food and he recognised me. He said he remembered you and I had sat outside at the same table two nights running and he was so happy I had bought the kids to visit his restaurant. Another moment where I was acutely reminded that we had left our mark with fondness as a couple 12 months prior; the complete unfairness of you not being here feels like a punch to the gut.

Tori said it was the most amazing birthday she had ever had in her life, making memories never to be forgotten.

I cannot imagine I will ever go back to be honest. It is just not the same without you.

18th May 2024

Seven months.

Yesterday the kids and I visited Portovenere; this town was our favourite and we planned to come back here and stay longer.

Yesterday I lit another candle for you inside the old church up near the cemetery on the hill where we visited 12 months ago nearly to the day. And I sat down on one of the wooden benches inside and broke down.

I wanted to tell you the guy playing the harp was still here and he wanted me to send him photos we took of his cat who was now gone. The foccaciaria where we had the amazing pillows of the softest focaccia in Italy and the most delicious Farinata was still just as amazing. That there was a restaurant with freshly made plant-based ravioli for me that was divine. That I bought the small barrel olive oil and local caperberries from the same place as last time.

I just wanted to tell you.

Today I travel to Venice, another trip into our memories, another part of this healing journey I am on.

Seven months goes by so quickly and yet it seems so long and heavy on my heart.

24th May 2024

Another milestone of sorts. On Wednesday the kids and I left Italy bound for Nice and nearly missed the plane. Still cannot work out how that happened as we were in the departure lounge waiting patiently to board. Boy did we get a talking to as the five of us ran towards the gate herded by an irate flight attendant. You passed a week before we were to fly into Nice last year, so it hits hard that you never got to experience this piece of paradise with me where the water and the sky blend together in the most magical blue as far as the eye can see.

Today my boys and their girlfriends fly back to Brisbane. That was an emotional parting outside the hotel as we clung together, the girls looking on with tears in their eyes. Their taxi pulled away and I walked in the opposite direction towards my next hotel dragging my suitcase behind, alone.

Spousal Grief

I had some bad headaches, body aches and a bloated stomach the first night in the new hotel. I woke up at around 3am and asked you to please help with the pain. You appeared and wrapped me up in pure white and golden light again and again drew the pain out of my body. I then fell into the deepest sleep and woke around 9am and felt so much better.

I know you are here in spirit helping me when I ask for it.

I miss you physically.

25th May 2024

I woke up feeling worse, head full of a cold and a fever so planned an easy restful day. I went down for breakfast then over to the markets to stock up on fresh fruit and juice, found a chemist then sat next to an elderly French man on a park bench overlooking the ocean, taking in some vitamin D, munching on my garlic and people-watching. I pretended it was you beside me sitting in an easy comfortable silence breathing in the sea air instead of focusing on how you would have gone off to get the things I needed to help me feel better. Back to the hotel for a few hours' sleep and then announced to the empty room that I would climb a mountain behind the hotel to the castle and waterfall beyond. This is where you would tell me I must be delirious and should rest more, but you're not here to stop me on my crazy quest. The room is closing in on me on my own so I must leave. It was breathtaking in so many ways and just what I needed.

Seeking Sunshine in the Shadows

I went back into the old town and had a coffee and a wander and found the Cathedral, crazy busy with a noisy group all dressed up for photos at the altar. I continued wandering just being in the moment until I found myself back at my hotel yet again. Had a shower, threw on some fresh clothes and went off in search of food. Found an amazing tiny little restaurant and tried my best to eat slowly but without you to talk to I gave up and it was all over within 30 minutes. It stays light here until 9.30pm so around the headland I went to walk off dinner and to find where the superyachts sail in and out on my back doorstep. I sat looking out over the ocean and saw clouds shaped like angel wings which were so beautiful and I imagined you looking down at me.

Tomorrow I will check out the marina and then I am off to retreat the day after. Looking forward to some gentle healing in a safe space.

I went to bed quietly reflecting on the journey. Solo travelling is empowering when you choose it and downright lonely when you don't. Being sick isn't helping right now, but I'll find my groove.

26th May 2024

Yesterday's small cruise ship is replaced by a much larger one in port. Along with the number of superyachts and run-of-the-mill yachts, it is quite spectacular to see. The Grand Prix is on so it is no wonder there are so many in every port. If you were here I know we would be on a train to Monaco to check out the rich and famous, but instead I walk along the wall towards the lighthouse and hang out at the end for a while as a domestic

Spousal Grief

dispute appeared to be going on in French. A man had a woman trapped with his arms locked onto the railing either side and she had arms crossed looking quite uncomfortable so I smiled at her and stayed close in the hope that my presence might diffuse things and let her feel less alone in whatever was playing out. I am sad for this couple in so many ways, but mainly because they don't value what they could have.

I am still sick babe but on the mend, so had a nap and read on my balcony and then off to dinner for Indian food to nurture the healing vibes. I find I am not the only woman on my own, two others followed me in to each eat a solitary meal as well. It makes me feel less alone, but at the same time it highlights how lonely I am without you. Early night as I have a train to catch in the morning!

27th May 2024

Woohoo, today is retreat day. I am excited as I really need the company of a small group of like-minded women in a spiritually healing setting eating amazing plant-based high-vibration food and engaging in soul-nurturing activities.

I have successfully navigated the train system without you, very similar to Italy really so I am full of confidence, so much so that an American woman approached me for assistance. I laugh as I say I don't really know what I'm doing and she tells me that I look like I do.

I arrive in Toulon and the facilitator is not the calming presence I expected. She is harassed and unnecessarily tells me that the

Seeking Sunshine in the Shadows

chef/masseur/yoga/meditation person had pulled out two weeks prior but that they had been replaced. Sadly it was apparent at that first day's meals the lovely young replacement could not cook. That's being polite. I was also informed that there would be a couple attending and the man 'had to have meat' which was going to be allowed for the first time on any of her retreats, but would be cooked outside. This was all contrary to what I'd been promised. It turned out to be the least of my concerns.

At the first mid-afternoon lunch the male said with much hostility, 'I don't have a problem with vegans as long as they respect me'. How would you imagine the facilitator responded to this antagonistic display by a guest on their healing retreat? Totally oblivious apparently.

Babe you would have lost your shit at the food on offer, you would have gone into the kitchen and fed yourself. You would have told this man to pull his head in peppered with some choice profanities. You would have said we are leaving as 'life is too short for this sort of BS'.

I was definitely thrown and mainly focused on my distress that there was a couple there. I am no longer part of a couple, not by choice but by your death. It is so triggering for me and I chose this retreat knowing there were no men or couples attending. I should have left then and there but I am ever the optimist and give the benefit of the doubt to people hoping they will choose kindness. For me it was not a great start to a healing journey and a pre-cursor of what was to come.

Spousal Grief

28th May 2024

Today is a new day so time to re-set from yesterday. But …..

The way the day unfolded, it is so ridiculous you can't make this shit up. I resorted to journaling about it as if I was a character in a well-known period Netflix series.

Following an unappetising breakfast I offered to cook. I needed to eat. I needed to attempt to stop the trainwreck I could see unfolding. After some convincing the facilitator took up my offer of dinner chef and she decided to swap our planned outing and said she would go and purchase food.

Then I asked to speak to her about my concerns, which one of the other guests had already addressed from her perspective. Apart from the broken promises of the food, the programme not being followed, the hostility by the male attendee, the space not being a safe, supportive one to share, my biggest upset was how triggered I was seeing a couple on retreat and that she thought that was ok to spring on me with no option to cancel. It really upset me. She was very aware of your death and the trauma surrounding it and that I was grieving and I explained how my time with my children and their partners in Italy brought me great joy. I also had moments where I had to excuse myself and go to my hotel room and cry because of the reminders that I am no longer a couple. Her response was, 'You need to get over it'. To say I was shocked is an understatement. I kept my cool and calmly said, 'I won't get over Ryan's death, I will work through it, but not now, that's not why I'm here, this is meant to be a healing space and there was not meant to be a couple here let alone a hostile male'.

Seeking Sunshine in the Shadows

I knew then and there that the ego was much greater than the desire to take responsibility for the situation she had created.

The irony is not lost on me; that I don't have you here to support me, but that the reason I am here is because you're not.

29th May 2024

I may have lost my mind at this point and been dreaming of far-off lands to lighten the mood in the house in the South of France, this thing called a 'retreat'. I wish I had another name for it that was more accurate but nothing comes to mind.

Today was a fucking disaster. There is no other way for me to summarise it than those five words. The best part of the day was my pretty blue dress I had purchased in Nice for a lovely day in a medieval French village.

The hostility rose to a new level and I have become the unpaid cook, kitchenhand and waitress. I was prepared to have a healthy mature discussion at our 'planned' lunch over a glass of wine but that never happened as nothing was actually planned.

After cooking, serving and cleaning up dinner for everyone I ended up in quite a state trying to flee the house and the heaviness contained within. The compound was locked and no one could find the keys so I paced the perimeter eyeing off whether I could find a pole and vault over the high walls. I eventually escaped and sat drinking an Aperol spritz at the local village pizza restaurant, watching another solo woman downing shots with beer chasers and a bite of pizza from time to time. As I looked for answers in my solitude asking for your support from the other side, I couldn't help but wonder about this other woman's journey that had led her to the same place as me, clearly in distress. I left the restaurant feeling stronger than I have for a while, resolute in my decision to leave Toulon to continue looking for joy.

As I walked along the shoreline back to the house all I could think was 'we ride at dawn'. I was ready to battle for what was right. As I looked up into the sky the clouds parted and the moon shone through and I thanked you Ryan for always having my back.

30th May 2024

I left 'retreat' today and changed all my plans. The Cannes Film Festival had just finished so I decided my mission was to find Leo DiCaprio.

The Airbnb I booked last minute was the nicest I'd stayed in so far and once there I started to decompress from what had happened. A trauma expert adding to my trauma. At this stage I had so many emotions running through me but the added trauma was hindering my thought process.

I let it go for now and decided to enjoy what Cannes had to offer. The vibe of this town is something else, I am already looking in real estate windows for apartment prices. You would love it here.

Seeking Sunshine in the Shadows

7th June 2024

Babe, I never got to Greece. I can't even process it all yet. I was supposed to find healing but instead I am extremely disappointed and quite distressed when all is said and done.

I did get to see Menton on the border of Italy, thanks to a recommendation from a random German tourist. Whilst it is a very pretty town, it was probably the loneliest I've felt on this trip. There's a beautiful church where I lit a candle for you and ugly cried for a while. I have struggled to find the positives over the couple of days there to be honest. Surrounded by so much beauty it was still a lonely and challenging time.

At 10pm the night before I'm to leave my accommodation to re-join the road trip, the 'retreat' facilitator dismisses my upset and says she's going to bed. At this stage I'm in tears. She states she's 'specialised in trauma'! Well she's added to my trauma with her lack of awareness of what is appropriate, deflecting and laying blame elsewhere, not taking any responsibility, not creating a safe space on the retreat, all the while knowing why I was attending having lost you and needing healing. Among so many other things, she basically left me abandoned overseas on my own when it was untenable to continue with her as I was clearly lowest of her priorities. That's the kicker, she knew I was alone in Portugal when you died, I'm understandably struggling no longer being part of a couple and now I'm alone again, overseas and having to hastily regroup so I have a safe place to sleep. Lucky for me I'm the girl you want to make things happen in a crisis and I have the financial means to do so. That doesn't make it right though.

Spousal Grief

This is not over by a long shot.

9th June 2024

It's my last couple of days in Nice and I have moved hotels. I booked in for a massage to try to take some of the extra stress of the past couple of weeks away.

You will not be surprised that it was certainly an experience that could only happen to me.

First things first. The massage was incredible. Second only to the one I had in Rabat as part of my Hammam. I am still dreaming of repeating that experience.

The masseuse spoke very little English and my French was not up to the level of communication needed so with very few hand gestures we established how much clothing to remove and start laying face down. She was extremely skilled and I know I fell asleep a couple of times, I was that relaxed or drained, fine line on that one. Then she flipped me over onto my back, covered my eyes and got back to the task at hand. Quite suddenly she left the room, or at least I thought she left the room but I wasn't quite sure. So I lay there for a while, wondering if she was still there or not and I got the giggles. I coughed a few times. I made some odd noises to get her attention. I was sure I could hear breathing. I lay there for what I felt was like half an hour. I have no idea why I don't speak up in these situations but I don't. It's quite hilarious. So eventually I peeked out from under the eye covering and

Seeking Sunshine in the Shadows

I was alone. I got up and dressed and made my way out to reception. All she said was 'you sleep good'.

Another weird and wonderful encounter I'll chalk up to experience that is my life.

Another weird and wonderful encounter I can't share with you.

15th June 2024

Yesterday I had a grief day where I just let it happen instead of putting on a brave face.

It took me by surprise. In hindsight I know it's because of the added trauma from the retreat facilitator in France.

I yelled at you because you're not here.
I cried inconsolably because you're not here.
I am not ok.
But I am ok.
And that's ok.
Because I am human.
I miss you.

Chapter 9

Healing Begins With You

18th June 2024

8 months since you were living.
8 months since you died.
8 months since you were pain-free.
8 months since my pain started.
8 months of enough tears to fill a football stadium.
8 months of lonely days and even lonelier nights.
8 months of silent meals.
8 months of an empty seat in the car, on the couch, across the dinner table.
8 months of an empty space in our bed.
8 months since I heard your voice.

Spousal Grief

8 months since you heard mine.
8 months since I held your hand.
8 months since all those little things you take for granted as a couple just stopped, ceased to exist, never to happen again.
8 months since I lost my purpose, my passion, my drive.
8 months since our future ceased to exist.
8 months since our plans and dreams died with you.
8 months of missing everything about you.
8 months of wishing.
8 months of pain.

Because every day no matter how lazy or busy I am, no matter how much I laugh or how much I cry, I lose you over and over again.

When I think about the man on 'retreat' and his behaviour, and know he isn't half the man you were, it made me wonder yet again why you were chosen eight months ago and not arseholes like him. I shake my head and cannot work it out!

Tomorrow will be eight months and one day and I'll wake up and lose you again and then I'll get on with my day keeping busy and working out how my future looks.

One day I hope to find happiness again.

21st June 2024

I have to tell you all about this week, babe. After the recent shitty experience with the so-called healing retreat I went on,

Healing Begins With You

whilst in Nice I booked a shamanic healing with someone highly recommended to me for shortly after my return to Australia. I just wanted the negative energy from the terrible facilitator to be removed but I got so much more from the experience.

You know I am one who does a lot of self-care and healing, even before I lost you, and you were always so supportive of these rituals for me even though it wasn't something you were drawn to. I love the spirit world, reiki is a beautiful practice, I've seen many mediums and psychics over the years and I talk to my angels all the time including you now. I am also a very practical person … go figure.

This week's healing was the most incredible experience I have ever had. The woman I saw held space for my grief and trauma from losing you and then being let down and abandoned by that awful facilitator overseas. She was beautiful and cried with me. Then the healing began. It was like being in a meditative state lying under a warm blanket with an eye pillow to help me focus, she cleared blocked chakras, sang, used sound bowls on me, played a gong, shook rattling things, saged me, I could go on. The images I saw, the beautiful colours, the feelings, seeing the negative energy try to rise up and defeat me and then turn to ash, the animals and people who surrounded me, it was so beautiful.

I was telling Jet and his girlfriend Charlee about the healing session last night at our dinner date, and Jet was sure I was given magic mushrooms or something. As I was telling them, right at the end of the session, running upstream towards me in the same bright colours as the rushing river was a wild rhino

Spousal Grief

and the water was parting to let him through. He was huge and coming straight at me with his big horn. But I felt no fear, just watched how beautiful he was and he ran straight to me and slammed into me pushing his face into my right shoulder. This magnificent creature nestled into me and my embrace with this overwhelming feeling that he was home where he belonged. I said I don't know why the rhino, but I feel he is my totem animal or something. And then it was over, but I felt the rhino come with me and attach to my right shoulder just in front as protection.

Jet was looking at me strangely as I explained this part and said, 'Mum, it's Ryan on your right shoulder'. I said, 'Yes Ryan is always standing behind my right shoulder supporting me, but this was a rhino, not Ryan'. Jet very slowly said, 'Mum, Rhino was Ryan's nickname'. Boom!! How did I not make the connection? I never called you that but Jet remembered clearly that you told him early on when meeting my boys that was your nickname. When I got home from the restaurant I walked in the house and stood in front of your photo and said, 'Rhino hey, well played babe'.

I slept through the last two nights since, I feel so much calmer in myself and my thoughts. There were so many things we discussed before and after the healing that I have taken away, that are of great benefit to me.

And I now know what my tattoo for you will be.

24th June 2024

The beautiful gift from Liza and Brian to see Greg the psychic was put to use today and he was as amazing as Liza said he would be. You came through very clearly and it was a very emotional reading. You spoke of Spain, Barcelona and finally Portugal. Told of the rich dinner the night before you passed. About our travel plans of Uluru, Osaka, Japan. And then you cried telling Greg about your death, your heart, your oxygen levels, that you knew what was happening during the night. You clearly described every part of your passing, how your body moved, your face, your mouth. And you were gone so quickly. You are crying not from your passing but because you said I was the love of your life and you didn't want to leave me. You went on to talk about less intense details of your life and you as a person. The way your jaw clicked, the carpal tunnel in both hands, the accident in my car. Your battle with your weight, sleep apnea, smoking, heart blockage, all contributed to your passing.

In the spirit world you have been well-received as the lovely man you are. And you are with the black and white dog starting with L. The only time I saw you cry was when we had to help Lou over the rainbow bridge, now you are with him.

You spoke of my children, Max and his guitar, Craig my brother, Peter my nephew. Then you said you were cremated and I have your urn which is good, it is how you wanted it, it is what we talked about. It is to stay with me. The T is your mother and connection to New Zealand and how there were problems the last time you saw her. You are carrying a lot of baggage surrounding your family.

Greg moved onto details about me, my boys, my niece, and there was so much clarity in everything he said and many things to focus on for the future. He said I must find JOY. There's that word again.

25th June 2024

Today I look at your photos, like I do every day, and it hits me once again how I can't comprehend that you are no longer living, breathing, talking, walking, snoring, laughing. How is this possible!! Your photos look so full of life. I clearly remember everything about where each photo was taken, where we were, why we were there, how we felt.

I am exceptionally tired after last week's healing with Bebe. I felt energised, focused and calmer from the session but today I am drained so I nap.

I miss having you here physically particularly on these low-energy days, you always carried me, took up the slack, fed animals, cleaned litters, brought me tea, made dinner. Now it is me, only me.

11th July 2024

940 million kilometres gone again! Another lap around the sun for me, another year closer to one that ends in 0 …. I don't love those ones but I am also very aware how privileged I am. All I can say of the year that has been is FARKKKKKK! It could have

Healing Begins With You

been better, it couldn't be worse, it has been my toughest to date – not a challenge universe, you can pull your head in right now!!

I have learnt even more about myself this past year of my life.
I have muddled through.
I have continued living.
I have made plans.
I have taken action.
I have continued to love.
I have found joy where I can.
I have been vulnerable.
I have leaned on others.
I have stood up for others.
I have kept my integrity.
I have risen above adversity.
I have retained my sense of humour.
I am sure there is more, much more, but for today that is enough thinking.
It is just another day, but it is also my birthday!
Another first I get to live through without you beside me.

Chapter 10

The Quiet Reminders of Love

<u>18th July 2024</u>

Today is another 18th of the month since 'that' day.

9 months!
273 days!
819 meals!
Without you.
12 flights!
12 destinations!
9 train rides!
1 family holiday

Spousal Grief

Without you.
Numerous:
Hotels, Airbnbs, Homes
Taxis, Buses, Body massages, Reiki, Meditation, Shamanic clearing,
Facials, Headspa, Haircuts, Counseling, Naturopath, Psychics,
Acupuncture, Sound healings, Reflexology, Pedicures, Lunches,
Brunches, Dinners, Friendships, Birthdays, Anniversaries
Without you.
Moved house
Jasper gone
Oceans of tears
Without you.

What does this all mean?

Some things I have considered today as I sat at the airport waiting to fly to chilly Melbourne:

* No one can fully understand a life phase or experience they haven't lived through.
* Empathy and intelligence has limits.
* We only ever know our own experiences.
* There's so much I know, but none of it prepared me for this knowing!
* Everything is exhausting.
* Everything is surreal.
* Sometimes taking a shower was the best I could do.
* The passage of time feels different now.
* I now understand that death warps our perceptions.
* Facebook continues to shove memories in my face but can't show me the future.

The Quiet Reminders of Love

* Time is accelerating.
* For now I am a coffee drinker; it gets me out of the house and into the world.
* Music is soothing and life-saving.
* The c-word entered my vocabulary temporarily.
* I truly understand what it's like to have no fucks left to give.
* I tell my loved ones 'I love you' more than ever before.
* Touch in any form is important for healing, hence the regular pampering sessions.
* I can go days without speaking to another human.

I have learned all of these things plus much more in the nine months without you.

You were the person I could hold on to.

You were the person who was there for me.

You will always remain my person. No one can take that from me.

No one can really understand what they've got until it's gone.

Nine months without you.

And I am doing quite well right now, today.

Spousal Grief

22nd July 2024

I am in Melbourne and have spent time with my brother and his family since Thursday and today I am at my BFF's for the next week.

The first morning I took myself off for a trip down memory lane to see the huge changes to the areas I grew up in. So much development, I was a bit disoriented trying to work out my bearings as the farmland I lived on is long gone, dirt roads are major thoroughfares and there are three McDonalds within a few kilometres of each other when there was never even one before.

I had brunch on my own in a new cafe but in an area I rode horses through with my friends as teenagers and I realised that it was the first time since you passed nine months ago that I have not felt lonely or alone when eating out by myself. On reflection I think it is because I grew up here, I was single here, and you were never part of my life in Victoria as we met after I moved to Queensland a long time ago. So the feeling of someone or something missing just wasn't there. It gives me hope, time will tell if that's a false sense of security I am feeling.

29th July 2024

I have not cried once about you babe, since being here in Melbourne but today in the car silent tears started as Faye said she could imagine your cheeky smile and I told her how you got your fade haircut in Morocco at last. The tears fell and now I can't stop them. I am sitting on the bed in my room, our room, their spare room, trying to compose myself.

The Quiet Reminders of Love

I miss you so much and wish you were here to share life with as planned. It's time to go home.

31st July 2024

I am on the plane from Melbourne back to the Gold Coast and there's a family with twins in front of me. One twin is looking at me intensely and smiling. He won't stop staring at me. The mother turned and asked if I want to have a cuddle. His name is Gus. I took him and he curled up on me like he was home and immediately went to sleep. I held him for the whole flight and the thought popped into my head that you had sent this sign. In my head I had his date of birth being the 19th October, 2023 – the day after you died. I asked her how old he was and she said nine months, born 19th October. As the plane started its descent I handed him back to his mother to strap him in. He looked back at me and kept raising a hand towards me. His mother smiled and said, 'He really loves you'. It really was a beautiful experience.

3rd August 2024

Tonight as I get ready for bed I have the thought that I am not afraid of dying and no matter what comes after is irrelevant. It is who is left behind, they all move on pretty quickly. You are reduced to a name in a photo until the generations after you die out and no one knows who you are anymore.

So I am not ready to die yet. I want a long life, that I am clear about. But I am no longer afraid of death. It is my epiphany today.

Spousal Grief

18th August 2024

Ten months and I will always speak your name Ryan!! Rhino was the nickname you told us about when we met. I never used it. The rhino came to me in my shamanic healing as protector and settled in front of my shoulder and I knew that was the tattoo I was going to get to honour you in my life. Rhino now has a permanent place to help guide me through this next part of life and Jasper's paw print is on my left arm in his memory too.

20th August 2024

It is official, I am going to write a book, the book that friends and family have encouraged me to write. The book about losing you. The book will be about surviving the first 12 months without you. I have journalled since the day you died, so it is certainly no big stretch to dump all of those words into a document and then set about formatting it. Writing is cathartic for me, which is why I wrote down anything and everything, I needed it to spew forth out of my head as I thought I might go crazy from the overwhelm of it all. After speaking with my sister-in-law last month and finding out she is writing a book of fiction, it was a great boost to get some guidance from her. And this has led me to today. I have attended a half-day seminar about becoming an author and I am taking the plunge and making this happen. There is the ever-present wish that you were here to share this leap of faith with. There is also the sad reality that this book would not be written if you were here.

The Quiet Reminders of Love

29th August 2023

Today the date seemed so familiar and has been niggling at me for most of the day. I have been busy out on the roads and put the craziness down to Mercury Retrograde finishing, but the heart knows what the heart knows and won't be ignored. Emotions have run very high, songs in the car have had tears streaming down my face and my heart hurting.

All of a sudden I know why. One year ago today we left on our biggest adventure yet. The one we pulled forward because 'why are we waiting'.

It is a year since you left Australian soil not knowing it was to be your last time.

If we had known then what I know now would we have stayed home? Would we have done things differently? Futile questions of course, but that doesn't stop them from forming in my head.

Grief continues to remind me she lives inside me now along with all the other emotions humans get to experience, good and bad.

Another first on this journey. The other firsts are to be expected I guess, the first Christmas without you, birthdays, Easter, anniversaries but this one crept up on me out of nowhere. I hadn't expected it.

Spousal Grief

12th September 2024

I had my one-on-one author mentoring today and it was very insightful. What is extremely important to acknowledge to myself as I write this book is looking back and seeing how far I have come since 'that day'. It is sobering, comforting and encouraging all at once. The amount of words I have journalled at different times is the true indication of how time allows other thoughts in, grief is no longer all-encompassing.

It is of equal importance that I can acknowledge that my love for you has not diminished, I just have room for living alongside that love and loss of your physical presence, that will never change. It's like death has taken away your physical body, your death felt so final but now I see that love doesn't die and I think that was a very real fear somewhere along the line, forgetting the love as life takes over, but it's simply not possible which is a calming realisation.

14th September 2024

Had such a restless night last night and I definitely know why. I've been invited to a birthday dinner for a beautiful friend of mine at a gorgeous restaurant about 30 minutes from home. It is somewhere you and I would love to try, beautiful ambience, interesting food, high end chefs.

I am accepting that you are not here to come with me but …. I am so triggered.

The Quiet Reminders of Love

There will be seven couples …. and me.

Me driving alone.
Me sitting alone in a group.
Me choosing dishes alone whilst they share with each other.
Me leaving alone.

That is where the anxiety hits hardest now. I just cannot do it. I have avoided going for dinner with couples because I end up sad and teary. Once the thought hits the strain to hold back tears, smile brightly and frantically try to think happy thoughts is draining and not always successful.

I need to find a way to dine with couples, but not tonight.

I have sent an honest message to my beautiful friend explaining why I need to bow out at the last minute, I trust her with this truth, my truth, and know she will not totally understand as she has not lost her person, but will empathise with my state of mind and forgive me, such is our friendship.

So much gratitude to have such friends in my life who support me and don't say things like: it's been long enough, you need to get over it, you need to push through it, and other well-meant but damaging words.

I read something the other day and it was so perfect. The things people say because they don't understand but want to be caring and the alternatives that mean so much more.

- Everything happens for a reason – *replace with* – Things happen and some things are random and devastating.
- They wouldn't want you to be sad – *replace with* – They would completely understand why you are heartbroken and they would feel the exact same way if roles were reversed.
- You just need to focus on the positive – *replace with* – You just need to find the people and places that don't make you feel like you have to hide your pain and remind you that it's ok to feel it all.
- They're in a better place – *replace with* – They're gone and it's so unfair.

15th September 2024

I am standing in the bathroom and feel an overwhelming pull to finally open the black bag.
The black bag with the sealed box.
The sealed box with the urn.
The urn with your ashes.

As I place the black bag on our bed, I lift the box out of the bag. At the exact same moment Zima races across the room onto the bed and somehow entangles herself to the black bag and as she leaps through the air off the other side onto her cat tower the black bag detaches and settles on the bed. I watch her jump back onto the bed and settle on top of the black bag and start grooming.

The Quiet Reminders of Love

I shake my head and get the tape off the box and I am feeling very calm. I reach inside to remove the top protective packing and lift out your urn that is inside another bag. This bag is dark green, my favourite colour.

There is a tag with your name attached to the green bag, the same green as the new linen I have on our bed. I look at the wires wrapped around the urn itself, they look official and not easily removed, I know they have been placed there by a government official. I will work out how to remove them one day. That day is for another time. The urn lid is loose and I can hear your ashes, your body, move inside. I can see how they will pour easily into the ocean upon release.

The thought of releasing you anywhere.
One day.
Not today.

I put you and your green bag back on the shelf next to the ashes of Jasper and Lou. I am getting quite a collection.

I shed tears and lay on the bed watching Zima sitting firmly and territorially on your black bag. Not a day to battle her by the look in her eyes.

I look at the calendar and count the days and more tears spring to my eyes. What are the odds that today of all days I am back to counting days again?

It's no coincidence. I don't believe in them.

333 days.
333 is my mum's angel number. You know this.
333 is my tattoo above my heart.
333 is a sign.
333 is a comfort.

I wipe my tears away and go back into the bathroom and finish getting ready for the day.

17th September 2024

You made your presence known again today. Not sure if it is because tomorrow is another significant date or because you took advantage of my relaxed state of mind. As I write this I guess it is a bit of both.

I haven't had a massage for some time and couldn't get in for a couple of weeks so was very glad I had my extra long facial booked today. It was time for some pampering. Touch is such an important part of my self-care because your absence means everyday human touch is gone too. It is not a sexual thing of course, it simply gives a boost to my emotional and physical well-being.

Today was the best facial I can remember. The day spa I go to is all about care for the client, the earth and the skin. Foot, hand and head massages form part of the facial and I sank deep into a state of relaxation. As I emptied my mind your face appeared so clearly and each touch from the beauty therapist was like you were the one actually carrying out the actions, your eyes never left

The Quiet Reminders of Love

mine, but they also put pressure on each stroke of the face brush, each wipe of the cleanser, and the weight of the mask over all parts of my face were you. It is difficult to explain if you haven't experienced these things, but you were there with every step.

As the therapist finished the treatment with gentle words bringing me slowly back into my body with the pure sound of the singing bowl, a vivid bright white light shone out from my third eye and you were gone and in your place was a beautiful feeling of peace.

I walked out floating on air and as I sat in the car refocusing to drive home, a message pinged on my phone offering a last-minute massage appointment tomorrow. That is a resounding yes! Thanks babe.

Chapter 11

Putting a Name to the Pain

18th September 2024

Photos of us one year ago in Tarifa in Spain are bringing back such poignant reminders of how we felt, what we saw and what we planned. One month later you were gone.

I am not sure how I picked this town as being part of our travels, it seemed natural as there is a ferry service that goes to Morocco but there are also more common ferry routes from other towns in Spain. As we peered out the window from our bus, the stop before we got here worried me slightly but we were committed to the journey. Then we got to Tarifa and the bus station was a tiny shed and two taxi parking spaces but only one taxi. I turned to you laughing and said with some trepidation, 'Don't worry, it's a stopover, we're only here two nights'. A random guy wanted to share a taxi with us and was keen to overshare his previous trips here. As the only taxi disappeared off down the street with another group of people and no other taxi was coming any time soon, we set off on the 1.2km walk in the heat following the GPS into what looked like a boring, lifeless, industrial town. Eventually we walked up to this ancient wall with stunning arabesque gates and wandered through into the old town. What a magical place. We found our boutique hotel and dragged ourselves up three flights of stairs to the top and were shown into the most fabulous accommodation in a heritage-listed building. We went back downstairs to the reception/bar/lounge and discovered the floors concealed historic holes where centuries before were stored food and drinks to keep them cold.

As we explored that first afternoon we found a colony of street tomcats and as they all gathered around me vying for attention you laughed and pointed at their imposing furry pompoms and said, 'Babe, are we coming back here to establish a TNR (trap neuter release) programme in the near future?' You know me so well.

The next day we set out on the whale-watching boats run by a whale conservation group from Germany. That sat well with me as we listened to how they had spent years tracking the swimming and migration patterns of all the whale species in the area and over this time their data had made such positive and lasting change to this busy shipping channel to ensure the boats were not impacting the lives of these gorgeous sea creatures. Upon learning how to volunteer I realised I'd need a crash course in

German at a minimum and made careful note of this for the future.

We fell in love with this impressive little town in the two nights we were there and immediately planned to return and spend much more time here.

My thoughts return to the date. Today is 11 months since you took your last breath.

The start of this Rocky Horror song is stuck in my head the past couple of days – 'It's astounding, time is fleeting, madness takes its toll'.

Sometimes I feel I am going mad.

19th September 2024

It is my mother's birthday today. She would have been 88 years old but instead it's 25 birthdays without her. I reflect on the three closest deaths in my life being my parents and you. All three were filled with trauma. My mother died suddenly and it was a shock. My father died suddenly and it was a shock. You died suddenly and it was a shock. I wonder briefly on the generational trauma or death trauma that has followed me in this life. There is something to this, but I put that thought away for another day.

As I do most years I've kept busy today. Met up with an old school friend for coffee first up and have a great catchup. Then onto a salon for my eyebrow tattooing appointment. I love the

Spousal Grief

shape and I know they'll settle but I do giggle picturing your initial reaction. You'd raise your bushy eyebrows and ask me gently if I am happy with them, and when I say yes then you'll move on to something else. As long as I was happy then you were supportive.

Opening my email I find there is one from your sister .... after all this time. I am surprised as I blocked her from my life but I didn't have her personal email so this one has made its way past the boundaries I have put in place. It initially jolts me to see the name and even more so the topic which is clearly a typo, but irritates me nonetheless – the lack of care to get it right. 'Plague for Ryan' it reads. So quickly scanning the contents I see it is an excuse to have another dig, how I've kept your death certificate, ashes etc for myself. She is informing me that she is getting a memorial plaque made for you to put at the beach and wants to know if I want my name on it or if it should just be from 'your family'. If you were alive I know you'd be appalled by a plaque; it is my initial reaction to imagine your reaction, but you're not here to say what you think so that's a mute point. What I do know is that the wording has 'partner' one level above friend but well below son, brother and uncle and my name is tacked on at the end. Another confirmation of their views of where I sit in importance in your life and now in death. Is it hurtful? Yes. Does it send me into an emotional spin? Not anymore. I close the email and shake my head. I won't be responding to this either. My inner circle is hallowed ground and my time is sacred.

In hindsight, knowing what I know now, I should have spoken up very early on and been very clear that I am your next of kin and I'll arrange your memorial how I know you wanted it. Your family are more than welcome to attend but should do their own get-together to celebrate your life if they are not comfortable being guests and not in control of the content of the day. The outcome would have been the same except I would still have contact with your dad – it makes me sad that he is missing out on our visits and talking about you, your travels, your life's final chapter. But instead, I fell back into my pattern of keeping the peace initially until I emotionally couldn't any more. But you don't know what you don't know until you do know. And what I do know is I am comfortable with how I conducted myself through the toughest period of my life as I grappled with the shock and aftermath of your unexpected death.

21st September 2024

Fatigue has been overwhelming the past few days. Last night I was extremely reluctant to go to bed even though I was exhausted. It is because you're not here, you're never coming back. The thought pops into my head that I am just killing time, I am on the treadmill day in day out. I am just existing. I am not living. That is deflating, defeating.

I wasted the whole morning on the couch. I have a headache, I am foggy, I just want to sleep and wake up a year from now feeling better. So I head back to the bedroom to close my eyes and forget this waking nightmare, this empty ache.

The pile of dirty clothes near the door stare accusingly at me. I stare back and then look over at the pile of clean clothes at the end of the bed. I ignore both piles and climb into bed. I know it

Spousal Grief

is a week since I put new sheets on the bed, and I should change them today. I don't. Instead I crawl over to the other side where you should be, where the sheets are clean and fresh because no one has slept in that spot and I lay there and I cry. I wake up with a worse headache because I am so dehydrated but I do not care. I look at the ceiling fan and see the dust and think to myself, what is the fucking point?

Extreme anxiety has hit. Until this moment I thought I was long past the nausea, the racing heart, the feelings of panic. But it is clear I am not and it is back to punish me.

24th September 2024

Tonight as I light your candle in front of your picture and talk to you, like most nights, I ask myself how it is possible that you are dead. It is such a difficult thing to accept. We were on holiday, travelling, having the trip of a lifetime, plans made for the next day, then in the blink of an eye you do not exist anymore. I shake my head and a small part of me cannot comprehend it. I don't even know how to explain exactly how this feels inside my head, my heart and my gut or what can set me off on this spiral. A song in the car, your face on my phone screen, the front door Volcom mats of yours. The cupboard where only my clothes now hang, your surfboard in the spare room I simply cannot part with yet, hanging up your t-shirt I now sleep in. Even your mobile phone charger I still use and won't let a living soul borrow as I don't want it broken because if it dies it is another part of you I lose hold of. A bloody charger has me all possessive and territorial.

Putting a Name to the Pain

It's so very difficult to accept even knowing it's true.

26th September 2024

Every day this week so far I have taken myself off for brunch or lunch alone. I am trying to make this my new normal. I hate it because I didn't choose it but I do it anyway, otherwise I'd sit inside the house 24/7 not seeing anyone, not speaking to anyone, not being part of the world.

I am tired.
Of not sleeping.
Of sleeping.
Of feeling tired.
Of manic activity.
Of sloth-like non-activity.
Of walking around with no purpose.
Of laying on the couch.
Of going through the motions.
Of proscratinating.
Of avoiding.
Of Groundhog Day!

I slept for two hours this afternoon even though today I achieved nothing. Yesterday I got so much done.

I know crying fatigues me. I know it dehydrates me and that compounds my fatigue.

Spousal Grief

I sit on the couch eating another meal off my lap on my own.
I imagine you laying on the couch watching television.
I turn off the TV and go to bed.
Another day over.
Another day of existing.

27th September 2024

I wake up and the word pops into my head unannounced; I finally have a name for how I feel each day ... DREAD! A feeling of great anxiety and fear. I don't like it, feeling this way. It is not all the time but it is there bubbling away just below the surface ready to spring into action without notice.

It makes me incredibly sad.
It makes me cry a lot.

Once the tears subside so does the feeling of dread. I relax into it. I know it has tucked itself away, resting, building strength to resurface again tomorrow. I sit with it now, letting my mind wander, allowing it some space to talk to me, to tell me why I am feeling this way more this week than previous weeks.

Some thoughts come through with clarity and others are fuzzy.

I dread Groundhog Day. I like variety otherwise boredom sets in and I fall into bad habits. I dread I will be stuck reliving the same boring routine day in day out forever.

Putting a Name to the Pain

I dread your first-year death anniversary. Everything relates to the day you died. I feel a need to shed that relationship to a date but at the same time it is attached to me forever more. So I think I must find a way through it and remove the focus. Or I must find a healthy way of relating to it. I don't have the answers to that yet.

I dread your family, more specifically your mother and sister. Seeing their name on my phone, on email, fills me with dread. Because I know they want something I cannot give them, or more accurately I dread the nasty tone they use to try to get it. They clearly don't believe in using honey to catch a fly. Their language is a form of abuse and it has added to my trauma. I know it is part of who they are, I saw that very early on in our relationship. You warned me about them and yet I encouraged you to have a relationship with them. But now I have a choice, they are not my people. So I choose not to respond.

I went off for a massage today that I really needed after the morning of dread. Sat with my feet in a hot foot bath and cried. Got myself together before the therapist came back in the room.

Off to the podiatrist next. Of course I recall you booking me into one in Portugal for the day you died. I have avoided them since and my feet are paying the price. Strange how after nearly 11 months it is these seemingly inconsequential things that trigger painful memories.

Chapter 12

The Year That Changed Everything

<u>30th September 2024</u>

The eve before the month of October begins. I am a mess. I really cannot fathom how it has been a year already! Even though it was the most heartbreaking, surreal moment in time at the time, the first year has just snuck up on me.

In our widows' group, someone brought up guilt. I absolutely have felt guilt about your death. I have made peace with it mostly but it rears its ugly head occasionally.

My guilt is mostly about your last hours alive. I was so sleep-deprived as your snoring had been worse that week and different in the days prior so even though we had an amazing dinner and had such a really beautiful connection that evening, during the night I got up and tried to sleep on the couch with tissues stuck in my ears. I even Googled noise-cancelling sleep headphones and planned for us to go find some in the morning. You called out to me just hours before you passed, asking 'Am I bothering you' and I snapped 'Yes!' at you. As soon as I said it I knew it upset you, you hated your snoring disturbing my sleep. I am glad I went back to bed and tried to settle beside you or you would have died alone without me right there.

It breaks my heart that I was so short with you. In hindsight it is very confronting and sobering and could haunt me if I let it. It is awfully upsetting. The only way I really deal with this is knowing that our whole relationship is not summed up by that one moment of irritability or any other argument during our eight years together. Your snoring may have constantly disturbed my sleep but I wanted a solution, that is how important 'us' was to me.

9th October 2024

Nine days until the first-year anniversary of your death. I am completing forms for the detox healing retreat I am attending in a couple of weeks' time and working out which extra sessions are going to benefit me most. Of course the awful next of kin question comes up. It still makes my stomach twist, my throat close and tears spring to my eyes.

There is also another pattern emerging that I would like to break but I am not sure I will have any control over it. The health of our geriatric animals as they get closer to their end of life is coming up prior to any planned trip I have. Old man Murray is now not well and with our beautiful vet we are working on treating some concerning symptoms. As one resolves another takes its place. My gut tells me we are only marking time but whilst he is eating, drinking, toileting and looking for love and attention, his quality of life is good. I keep a close eye on the tiny changes only I see and will treat or make harder decisions accordingly. In the meantime I draw on some dark humour to deflect away from emotionally processing his probable upcoming demise. So as he has claimed the cardboard tray that Jasper's ashes were in to sleep on, I look at him and say, 'Oh well Muzza, you're next buddy, into the fire you'll go and I can add you to my ash collection'. He looks up at me and makes his adorable little peep meow to say he sees me and hears me. The slippery line between humour and insanity perhaps.

13th October 2024

361 days since that day. It was a leap year this year so in five days it will be 366 days. I feel stronger today than I was 361 days ago. I have less fear of many things today than I had 361 days ago. I laugh more often and more easily than I did even six months ago. And grief still visits every day to remind me not only of how much I have lost but how much I have loved.

14th October 2024

All week Zima has gotten herself out of bed and climbed onto her cat wheel at 11pm. Every night. She runs and it wakes me up. I call out for her to stop and she ignores me. She slows and starts walking really weirdly. I turn the light on and look at her. She ignores me further, stops walking and sits staring at a spot. I think it's you. I know it's you. You're encouraging her, I just know it. You're laughing about it for sure. So after a week of this the wheel is the last thing I dismantle every night and the first thing I put back up every morning. Grrrr.

15th October 2024

Three days to go. I am back to counting in days again. I have kept myself really busy this week and fully booked myself up to keep my mind off this final 'first' and it has been a good diversion.

Tonight I went down to see Max and Tori and they tell me they have booked lunch for us all on Friday and Jet and Charlee are taking the day off to be there. So kind and caring, a really nice gesture by the kids wanting to show support knowing it is going to be a hard day for me. I don't know how I feel about it though. Faye is coming up, which I love, but I know she won't care if I stay in bed curled up in a ball all day if that is the way it pans out. Now I am feeling under a lot of pressure. I have gone back upstairs and sat on the couch and burst into tears. Just the thought of it all is making me anxious. I don't want to upset them as it's their way of showing they care. I will have to see how I feel when the time comes.

Why can't you turn back the clock and undo everything and just be here and Friday just be another day?

The Year That Changed Everything

16th October 2024

You're certainly making your presence known at the moment more than ever. As I pulled into the drive earlier I see the rubbish bins are empty so I drive partway down the drive and open the car door. It naturally falls wide open as the drive here is steep. I leave it open and walk back up to get the bins. As I walk back down towards the car looking at the door I think I will have to walk the bins past the car single file as the door is blocking the way. As soon as the thought forms I watch the door slowly and firmly close. This simple movement defies gravity given the angle of the car on the driveway. There is no wind. I am not imagining things. Thanks babe for the help. Next week maybe you can bring the bins in themselves.

17th October 2024

How has today been, knowing your one-year anniversary is tomorrow? Hmmm …..

Tears first up.

Met my beautiful niece in Currumbin Valley to sit with a pot of herbal tea goodness beside calm flowing water. Conversation was easy and then it turned to you and as I was talking and both of us got teary Carly looked over my shoulder and said, 'OMG slowly turn around and look who's here'. I turned and on the chair behind me staring straight at me was a magpie. I love magpies, they're my favourite bird and Carly knows that and you know that, everyone knows that. At our old house I

Spousal Grief

had a magpie who used to tap on the windows for my attention and follow me and only me around the house, watching my every move from the outside. But Carly said there's no magpies anywhere here – he just flew in at that exact moment and had made a beeline for me. He sat for a while watching me as I spoke to him then flew low over me to a higher spot and turned and looked at me again for a few long moments before flying off. I don't know if he was there to show me reassurance or if it was you but it was certainly a comforting sign.

Then I headed to the airport to collect my BFF Faye. As I was sitting and waiting for the plane to land, there were more tears in anticipation which stopped before I drove to the pick-up point and we both busied ourselves with her luggage and getting in the car. I sense we both had the same idea of avoiding the emotions just yet. Her calming presence is a godsend and great distraction as we caught up on each others' lives since my July trip down south.

I sat up late after she went to bed and started sorting through photos of you and was surprisingly calm and quite emotionless, like I was looking in as an observer rather than the leading lady with my leading man.

As I hop into bed the dam bursts its banks and the floodgates open. I knew it was too good to be true. The calm before the storm, where grief has tiptoed around in the shadows looking for the inevitable chink in my armour and upon finding it, hits me square between the eyes and releases first a trickle and then a torrent of tears.

The Year That Changed Everything

Zima looks on and cries out loud at me, seeming to join in. That is a new thing for her.

Sleep time, need to recharge to face whatever tomorrow brings.

18th October 2024

Eerily dry eyed this morning upon waking. I am acutely aware of the date, the relevance, the marking of time. One year, you died one year ago today. That means I am entering my second year without you. I hadn't given that reality much thought.

For a full 15 minutes I lay in bed staring at Zima who is staring at the air, the space beside the bed, she is intense, looking up and down and around at this one area. She sees and feels you there.

My mind is quite empty of thought, is it protecting me, is this what self-preservation feels like? Perhaps. I feel tears spring to my eyes, I blink them away. I am thinking that I am not ready for that but at the same time I think I need to get it out before I face the day out there beyond the bedroom door, where the people are, where society lives, where others go about their daily lives oblivious to personal death and loss.

Then the tears flow. They gush out at first and then settle to a gentle flow. Gentle flow!! Interesting how that thought forms. Compared to what, the torrent of racking sobs that are all-consuming, that I am all too familiar with, maybe. And finally I chastise myself, as if I can control grief. She has a mind of her own. She is a free spirit and will not be told when and how to behave.

Spousal Grief

Faye and I run errands and go to meet up with the kids for lunch. I have issued instructions that I do not want anyone toasting you at lunch unless I bring it up. I know I am being selfish, but I do not want to cry at the table. So lots of small talk, lots of good food in a beautiful setting, with beautiful family, without you.

My phone rings as we are finishing up. Emma (our dog) has got out and a neighbour has her in his yard. I am concerned how a nearly 17-year-old dog with limited mobility can escape. I drive there and get her home and we scour the perimeter but there is nothing open, no holes dug, we cannot work it out. At the back of my mind I know her dementia is the culprit, she is confused and her need to find something familiar has overtaken her thought process and she must have found a weak spot to break out. I put the boys to work on making the gates and fences more secure. As I think more about it, I face the reality that her time here earthbound is drawing to a close and I am going to have to make the hardest but kindest decision that a human can for their furbaby and let her go. They say things come in threes. I can't really deal with that thought today.

I am suddenly exhausted and lie down for an afternoon nap. I wake up and look at the clock. The time is ticking away and it is nearly 4.50pm AEST. One year ago at this exact time you spoke your last words to me babe, telling me you 'weren't feeling right'. Then you were gone. I couldn't save you. I didn't possess any superpowers. My heart truly broke. And there are the floodgates opening wide up again and those racking sobs have arrived to claim me. I give in to the crash of the waves pounding on me and let the tears pour out of me.

The Year That Changed Everything

I think back over the past 12 months and realise that this is what surviving the first year without you looks like. It's not what I would have chosen. I used to think in life you are given the hand you can deal with, but I know this is not true. You deal with the hand you are dealt and that's what I am doing, it's what humans are designed to do.

I still can't look at a photo of you without disbelief, but I no longer cry at every photo, at every thought of you, at every mention of your name.

When we met I knew you weren't perfect but I loved you anyway. It turned out you were perfect for me.

Forever in my heart.

Reflection

26th October 2024

One year today I started the journey to bring your ashes home. Three flights, Porto to Lisbon to Dubai to Brisbane. I returned home a broken woman, forever changed.

Today I return home from a different journey. I came to this week-long retreat in Byron Bay to cleanse, to detox my body, to start to physically heal the damage that grief wreaks on one's self. I will not live this next chapter of my life as a shell of who I was. I have realised I am where I am supposed to be this week. I received so much more than I anticipated. I am vibrating at a higher level from this incredible experience and I leave here a changed woman, a newer, improved version of myself with a clear understanding of my life's purpose.

Personal and spiritual growth is ongoing, self-love and care is not a one-off transaction but a continuing practice.

Spousal Grief

I love and miss Ryan terribly, but I now understand that I am not the emotion, I am feeling emotions, so I cannot let them take up permanent residence. They must flow and ebb like the tides, be given the space and respect they deserve and then move on to allow other emotions to appear, be felt and then flow.

Namaste.

About the Author

Kylie was born in Victoria, Australia, and has always embraced a life rich in adventure and purpose. After a successful career in the corporate world, she followed her heart into the culinary world, opening her own restaurant and blending her love for food with the spirit of entrepreneurship. Now living on the beautiful Gold Coast, Kylie finds inspiration in her travels, food explorations, and the stories that connect people.

As a proud mother of two adult sons, Kylie cherishes the power of storytelling, especially after experiencing the devastating loss of her partner. Her journey of resilience and love for life shines through in her writing, where she brings warmth, humour, and vulnerability to each page.

Beyond the pen, Kylie is committed to her community, volunteering in animal rescue and using her culinary talents to prepare meals for charity and fundraising events. Her debut book is a raw, heartfelt journey that reminds readers of the strength found in vulnerability and the beauty of honouring life's moments, even amid profound loss.

Notes

Spousal Grief

Notes

Spousal Grief

Notes

www.ingramcontent.com/pod-product-compliance
Lightning Source LLC
Chambersburg PA
CBHW030220100526
44584CB00014BA/1379